# *The* FINAL CLOSET

## *The Gay Parents' Guide for Coming Out to Their Children*

### RIP CORLEY, C.S.W., A.C.P.

editech press ■ miami

First Edition
© 1990 by Rip Corley

Library of Congress Cataloging-in-Publication Data

Corley, Rip, 1946-
   The final closet: the gay parents' guide for coming out to their children/Rip Corley.—1st ed.
      192 p.      cm.
   Includes bibliographical references.
   ISBN 0-945586-08-6   :   $8.95
   1. Gay parents—United States.   2. Children of gay parents —United States—Family relationships.   3. Parenting —United States.
I. Title.
HQ76.3.U5C66      1990                          89-82740
306.874—dc20                                        CIP

Printed in the United States of America

This is a revised edition of *The Last Closet: A Gay Parent's Guide for Coming Out to Your Children* (Exposition Press of Florida, Pompano Beach, 1987, 153 pp.).

# The FINAL CLOSET

# Table of Contents

# Preface

This book is the product of over 15 years of working in the field of psychotherapy and family therapy with a special emphasis on and dedication to the gay and lesbian community. I am the main author of this work, am gay, a licensed psychotherapist and Certified Social Worker-Advanced Clinical Practitioner. I am a gay parent only in the sense of having served in a helping capacity to bring dozens of gay and lesbian parents and their children into a closer, more honest and open relationship through the coming out process. Most of the contributors to this book have been gay parents. There are lesbian mothers and gay fathers who valued their relationship with their children enough to take the often times frightening and sometimes risky step of coming out to their children. It is those parents who have honored me by allowing me to share in that process.

The main contributing author, M. Deborah Gilboy, is not lesbian; however, she is a parent, a psychotherapist, and a loving person who believes in, and in fact insists on, people developing "real" relationships. She is the founding Executive Director of Share Centers (Sexuality, Human Awareness, and Relationship Education).

Collectively, for two years, she and I and countless consultants in many disciplines have labored over this book, its potential impact and even its political implications (some of which may have a backlash effect).

Recognizing the tendency of human beings' preference to align themselves in groups, we were careful in our choice of consultants. Knowing that we would be using "we" in a generic sense in the text, she and I did not want to use consultants who would be concerned about "identification by association." Rather, we wanted consultation from experts in the "let's help each other feel better about themselves" business to assist us in this book. To date not one of them has asked us if their names would be acknowledged in the book and if so, to identify them as gay or straight. We do know this: we can identify them as very human.

We also are aware of the limitations of our English language and equally to the sensitivity of the inclusive language issue. To facilitate reading and clarity, we frequently have used the term gay in a generic sense, meaning male or female, the same spirit goes for the generic "he." We have made an attempt when appropriate to split the examples using a lesbian situation one time and a gay male in other situations in the spirit of fairness to each group.

We bring two perspectives to this book. The first is from our experience as psychotherapists who have achieved an appreciable level of expertise in the mental health field, especially as it relates to the gay and lesbian community. The second, and more important perspective, is that we are trying to meet the innumerable requests from gay and lesbian parents for help in the coming out process.

A part of this book is designed to have the thrust of our mental health experience behind it as a guide that has worked well for several hundred clients. The other thrust of the book is to meet a real need in the gay and lesbian parents community to have this issue addressed, not as a clinical anomaly, but as a real compassionate human concern. We have tried and indeed continue to try to be a part of this community participating in the process of human growth and understanding. We certainly do not experience ourselves as being observers and reporters. We feel a very close tie to every gay and lesbian parent we have assisted in this process. We have cried many painful tears with them and shared in unmeasurable joys of becoming a whole family through this process.

We beg your indulgence while reading this guide if we occasionally come across a little clinical at times. It is a hazard of our training and professions. Also we ask your understanding if we occasionally treat the coming out process too casually, as if it is something you "just do." We realize it is a process that takes time, energy, and some risking. We applaud you, the gay and lesbian parents, for wanting to create a more real relationship between you and your children by reading this book.

# Introduction

**"D**addy, are you and Mommy ever going to get back together?"

"No, son, we're not."

"Daddy, do you make love with the man you live with the way you and Mommy did?"

From the mouths of babes come some of the most profound questions. The above is from the seven-year-old son of a recently divorced father who is gay—that being the basic reason for his divorce.

This scenario crosses the mind of every gay parent at some point in the coming out process. The question is one of whether to tell or not. If so, how and when?

Many gay parents erroneously assume if their children want to know, they will ask. Let's look at that assumption. Remember when we were children, curious about so many different things? Some things we felt completely safe to ask about, like why does the light come on when I flip the switch? On the other hand, there were some things we felt insecure in asking, like what do you and Mommy do in the bedroom making funny noises with the door closed?

Those subjects about which our parents demonstrated an easy going, supportive attitude, we would openly question. Those subjects our parents hedged around or avoided, we were uncomfortable in questioning. During our childhood, we frequently took cues from our parents about the safety of certain subjects. Similarly, your children will take cues from you about the openness and safety of certain subjects, especially your homosexuality.

Now consider homosexuality, with all its connotations (mostly negative) which your child learned as he grew (grows) up. Suppose there is something going on in your life that leads your child to believe you are gay, yet he has never heard you talk about it. Nevertheless, your child asks himself if Dad is that horrible, deranged, immoral creature he heard about on television or from his school chums. Even though your child is curious about certain lifestyles and partner choices, he will ask you direct questions only if he is very adventuresome.

Some parents assume their children know they are gay shortly after they—the parents—begin to show signs of a gay lifestyle. In our experience, this is generally true. Not every child will immediately conclude that gay behavior equals gay parent, but it does not take long for your child to put the evidence together and come up with a fairly accurate picture.

Chances are your children already know something's up. This understanding, however, is limited by age and ability to comprehend complex concepts like lifestyles and relationships. Remember, too, that your children, during their early years, grew (grow) up with many of the same unspoken negatives we grew up with. They must draw their conclusions from that information—actually misinformation.

Fortunately, attitudes about sexuality in general are changing. Society at large is becoming more understanding in light of accurate information. If the general public's attitude about gays and our rights as parents is ever going to change, then first our attitudes about ourselves as gay men and lesbian women, and as parents, must change. This book is about becoming a happy gay parent, having a healthy relationship with your child.

# The FINAL CLOSET

# Attitudes About
# Being Gay

The following is an excerpt from a gay parent's suicide note. ". . . You know, it's a weird thing in wanting to tell. It's like—because it has to be kept a secret, it's something to feel guilty about. At this point, it's almost a sense of keeping one's integrity not to tell, but it's such a part of our total existence, our total experience, our total selves. I am so aware of the singularity of my existence, having to live this way. It's very bothersome. The craziness of having to have a secret life when you have no desire to be secretive, and that very essence guilt thrives. If you can't tell something, it must be bad, that feeling you know. It's such a weird way to have to live our lives . . ."

Fortunately, this person did not succeed in his attempt and is living today in a happy, healthy relationship with his partner and child.

If we are to pursue happy lives as well as fulfilling relationships with others, how is it possible when so much of our life must be spent in secret, especially when there is "no desire to be secretive?" Most gays have no desire to advertise or proclaim their sexuality, any more than heterosexuals do. However, heterosexuality is assumed. Short of coming out on your own terms, gay parents have few ways to share this information with their children. Since heterosexuality is assumed, especially if parenting

**3**

is involved, then being gay and a parent makes a situation that is awkward and hard to explain.

Every gay person has heard: "What you do in your own bedroom is of no concern to us. We don't want to know, so don't tell us." If we believe this is what we are about, then we've reduced our life and lifestyle to the sexual activity behind our bedroom door.

All of us know we are much more than a sexual object engaging in sexual activity. As strange as it may seem, there are asexual homosexuals who have little or no sex drive or interest—just as there are heterosexual individuals who are asexual. We must part from this idea that a person is homosexual simply because there is an erotic attraction to a person of the same sex. The truth is that the homosexual's lifestyle and behavior can be and usually is as all-encompassing as is the heterosexual's.

If gay parents are to have open, healthy relationships with their children, it is important that they demonstrate positive behavior in front of them. The same holds true for any parent, gay or straight. Think how it would have been if all we saw our parents do was to act rather estranged toward one another when we were around, as if their mutual affection was more like that of roommates than parents. Children typically growing up with this example of relationships or marriage go on to act this way in their own adult relationships. They frequently will have difficulty bonding as well as being sexual and intimate. Sometimes they have difficulty experiencing a sense of family and belonging.

During your coming out phase you may be faced with this kind of question: "Won't the display of even socially appropriate affection between same-sex partners cause your children to grow up gay?"

The tone of the question already has a negative bias—that growing up gay is bad. For now, however, we'll avoid getting into the discussion of whether it is indeed bad to grow up gay. Let's answer the question directly with a resounding NO! Modeling a positive lifestyle or relationship —gay or straight—in front of a developing child does not influence the child's eventual gender preference. (After all, most of us grew up in a heterosexual environment). We have evidence all around us that children growing up with gay parents have proven no more likely to develop homosexual tendencies than children raised by heterosexual parents.

Consider the gay parents you know who have grown children. The percentage of these children growing up to be gay is equal or just under the national average (more in-depth attention will be paid to this in a later chapter). The important point is that children model the quality of relationships they see their parents displaying—not their sexuality. It is unlikely they will mimic "same-sex affectional behavior" with a person of the same sex just because they see you or another gay parent display such behavior. For now, keep in mind that relationship formation, bonding and interaction has little to do with choice of your partner's gender. Granted, gender is always important in your choice of partners and lifemates, but it is only one component of how these choices are made.

If your child experiences discomfort, cover-ups and excuses from you about your being gay, he may well develop a less than wholesome attitude regarding you. Conversely, if your child experiences warm, genuine openness on your part, he will experience many lifelong benefits, no matter whether the environment be gay or straight.

# Do Your Children Know?
# Do They Have
# A Right to Know?

**M**embers of the organization Children of Gays said on a recent television talk show that an overwhelming majority of children of gay parents would want to know if their parents are gay. Many told their own stories; that for a number of years they were aware of a hidden part of their parent's lives. Some at first thought the parent's strange behavior was the result of a heterosexual affair that would soon lead to a divorce in the family. Others thought the problem was due to something they—the children—had done wrong. The majority eventually figured out what was going on, but were still influenced by outdated information about homosexuality with which they had grown up.

Though a few children were glad they did not know the truth until they had reached adulthood, most expressed bitterness for the years of the parent's unexplained distance. Having no honest information about the situation, these children felt robbed of the opportunity to work through this information and form a closer, more honest relationship with their mothers and fathers.

Does a child have the right to know that her mother is lesbian? Does she have the right to a real relationship with her mother based on honesty, positive parenting and love?

We believe both child and parent have the right, even

the obligation, to be available for an honest relationship: a child told nothing about her mother's homosexuality can only relate to a fantasized parental image based on deceit and misinformation, even though her mother's intentions may have been the best in the world.

This does not assume that every lesbian mother, upon revealing her homosexuality to her children, will be met with open arms and understanding. Love and understanding are the most frequent long-term result, but your child may at first feel a lot of immediate resentment and outright hostility. Many will feel burdened with the stigma attached to homosexuality. If this is your situation, this will be a very tough time. However, almost everyone works through those difficult and negative feelings. If the relationship between you and your child prior to coming out was loving and stable, then it will likely emerge victorious and continue to be the ongoing relationship. Those of you who unfortunately do not reach a successful resolution and who find your relationship further strained will at least learn your relationship needs more work. Perhaps it needed more work prior to coming out.

This work may be painful and unrewarding at first, but most parents who have gone through it say that just getting rid of the burdening dread of being "found out" made the experience worthwhile, regardless of the outcome. While finding the answer for yourself will be a risk-taking step, remember that a bad experience and outcome is the exception, not the rule. Usually the result is positive. Keep in mind that you are laying the foundation for a lifelong relationship.

Not telling your children may appear to be the path of least resistance, but it is not without high costs. If, for example, your child's upcoming summer visit cancels some long-term vacation plans with your partner, you may well feel resentment towards her. The amount of intrusion a lesbian mother experiences from her unknowing child reflects the amount of resentment felt by that parent. On the other hand, if you cancel your child's visit, she may feel resentment towards you because you and your "roommate" wanted to go somewhere together.

If you decide to come out to your child, you may be wondering when would be the best time. Several considerations are important: your child's age, maturity, custody issues, previous parent/child relationship, and the attitude of the non-gay parent.

Your child is never too young to experience a positive relationship. However, sharing specific information with your child should be more closely tied to her chronological and developmental age — chronological age is your child's actual age while developmental age reflects your child's emotional maturity. An entire chapter on how, when, and what to say is included later in the book. You are encouraged to refer to that section for specific examples. For now, we will more closely examine the other considerations.

If you have primary custody you will have an advantage because there are fewer outside influences that might interfere.

If your child's grandparents are influential, hopefully they are already knowledgeable, understanding and supportive of your lifestyle. If so, this is a plus, because your child will not feel all this information is a burden and secret she must bear alone. If her grandparents are not supportive, this situation needs to be discussed with your child. It also is another area of your life that is worthy of serious consideration. You may well decide to attempt to establish a positive and supportive relationship with your parents and in-laws. The larger your supportive family system is, the easier the integration of the coming out process[1] will be for you and your child.

---

[1]Please be aware coming out is a process that occurs over time. It is not a one-time announcement. None of us just came out over night. Be generous and give your children and family time to process your coming out.

We feel it is important for you to always refer to the non-gay parent in a supportive, non-judgmental way, whether the non-gay parent is supportive or not. Remember, good parental modeling is just good behavior—not a trade off (if you approve of me, I won't not slander you in front of our children).

If you are the non-custodial parent, coming out may be more difficult, depending on your relationship with your ex-spouse. If your relationship is good and your ex-spouse is supportive, there will be little difference between the experience of custodial and non-custodial lesbian parents.

Without that support and understanding, the non-custodial lesbian parent is assuming a larger risk when telling her children. Your ex-spouse may attempt to block the sharing of information.

The issue of homosexuality can be a problem if your ex-spouse uses it as a lever to withhold reasonable visitation rights (which ideally should be defined the same for gay or straight parents). In certain parts of the country, depending on the temperament of divorce courts, visitation could be hampered. It would be unusual today for judges to revoke visitation, sever parental rights or invoke supervised visitation; however, it can and does happen. Today's usual outcome is for the judge to enforce reasonable visitation. In certain cases he may require some psychological and sociological testing of you if homosexuality becomes an issue. Your ex-spouse may feel restricted visitation is in order due to his or her misinformation, ignorance or prejudices. It could be easy to manipulate the situation knowing the sentiment of many courts lean towards the non-gay parent. This might leave you with some unexpected and unusual consequences.

Even though it is the court's mandate to act in the best interests of minor children, that mandate is poorly served when volatile issues like homosexuality, with all its trappings, are argued in court. Again, we refer to the abundant research that happy, healthy gay parents in happy, healthy relationships will not have bad effects on their children. Similarly, an unhappy relationship full of discord will have bad effects on children, whether the relationship is gay or straight, single or married.

Getting counsel from your divorce attorney before proceeding to discuss the issue with your child may be helpful. This is not to say that given advice to keep quiet, you should withhold this information from your children. In this situation, however, tactful and strategic preparatory legal work might have to be done before coming out to your children. In some cases you will have to weigh the potential cost against the benefits. If it is likely that telling them will result in restricted or severed visitation, you may reconsider and postpone coming out until your children are older.

If this is your situation, we suggest the following to make the transition of telling easier at a later date. Write your children letters explaining your current feelings, as well as the reasons for your not coming out until they are older. Write several letters over the coming years, keeping current with your feelings at the time. Writing them as your feelings surface, be as candid as you can be and keep in mind both the current age of your children and their ages when these letters will be shared. Date the letters. Seal the envelopes and put them in a very safe place to be shared later.

One other relationship is noteworthy. Some couples—one of whom is gay, the other straight—choose to remain married and co-parent their children. If this is your situation, the decision about sharing this information with your children may be a joint one built on mutual love and support, probably the same type already holding the relationship together. We feel, though, that the ultimate decision of coming out or not should be the gay parent's decision. We hope some of the examples in this book serve as supportive guidelines in your decision-making process.

We encourage you to carefully assess your situation and use this delayed method only if the risks of coming out are unacceptable. This is not a good method if you are merely seeking a means of escaping the pain of taking responsibility for this important part of your life.

The parent/child relationship transcends any one point in time. A relationship, good, bad or indifferent, lasts for a lifetime. If your child is a minor and you do not have custody, this alone should not impoverish you or your child of a rich and rewarding lifelong relationship. The custodial parent has custody only as long as your child is a minor. Thereafter, your child is free to pick and choose her relationships as she sees fit. In that vein, efforts must be made to build warm, loving relationships between you, your children and the other parent, custodial or not.

Many children are separated from contact with the gay parent only because of the issue of homosexuality. If your child is from this type of divorced home, she may believe you care nothing about her—simply abandoned her—never knowing you had been forced out of each other's lives.

It is a travesty when "in the best interest of the child" she is robbed of a close parental relationship for reasons of misinformation, vindictiveness of the custodial non-gay parent or the misguided tendencies of some divorce courts.

Here is a message to the non-gay parent, custodial or not. The best interests of the child must always remain foremost in the parent/child relationship. The child undeniably has both a mother and father. In most cases your child spent enough time as a part of her nuclear family to have formed relationships of her own, unique and special to her, with each parent. The child therefore deserves the right to make her own decisions regarding continuation of relationships should the parents divorce. It is important that she base her decision on complete, accurate, up-to-date information. Anything less is a denial of her rights.

Other things should be taken into account if the non-gay parent is absent, deceased or otherwise disinterested in the parenting role, thus leaving you custodian of your child. There have been cases where grandparents or other blood relatives on either side of the marriage have attempted to gain custody of a minor child. In the presence of a good healthy environment, seldom does a transfer of custody happen. As time passes and attitudes change, it is less likely that these cases will come to trial.[2]

There will naturally be a number of obstacles your child will have to work through—knowing you are lesbian and understanding your lifestyle—especially if she lives with you, but no one lives in a clear-cut world where everyone has a set of parents just like everyone else. Some parents are much older—the age of most grandparents; some are grandparents now in a second parenting role; some are interracial while others have physical disabilities. These circumstances test a child's ability to adjust.

Consider the case of interracial marriages. The test has not been how well the children can adjust, but rather how well other adults and parents in our society can adjust. We all have seen how easily and successfully children can adjust to differences, given the chance and proper guidance. This task is easier if you give your children accurate information and make an effort to build a supportive family in which decision making has been taught and encouraged.

Remember, a relationship is for a lifetime. A feud based on prejudicial issues can affect your relationship for a lifetime.

---

[2]Risher vs. Risher . . . for complete text account of case refer to *By Her Own Admission* (Gibson, Doubleday, New York 1977).

# The Family Secret

Sharing this type of information with your children raises difficult questions: when to tell them and what to tell them. Refer to the section on age-appropriate analogies to get clear examples of language and case histories. These are only rough guidelines. Because of each child's uniqueness, different psychological ages for the same chronological age, a precise "what-to-say and how-to-say it" manual is impossible to outline. If family counselors or child psychologists experienced in this area are available, or if "telling your children" workshops are held locally, these are resources that can help you.

We address the gay custodial parent's situation first. This may be the easiest situation to manage because you will have the most control over the information your child gets. You can correct erroneous information as an ongoing process (even before coming out to your child) and you control the setting in which this sharing takes place.

In all situations, custodial or not, the information should be age-appropriate. Very young children have a limited capacity to understand complex issues. Timing is important. Sharing with young children should not be done during times of major upheavals; moving from one school or town to another, during the divorce, etc. Remember, coming out may be taken as bad news by your child. Unless he already knows and sharing is simply the confirmation of a previous assumption, your child suddenly must say good-bye to many of his presumed fantasies; e.g., "Mommie will get married again" or "I won't be the odd kid on the block with only one parent," etc. Saying good-bye to the relationship between parents (assumed or otherwise) is stressful for a child, requiring time and understanding to grieve its passing.

The child should be assured that the divorce had nothing to do with her, the non-custodial parent is a good person/parent and that her relationship with her other parent should still be enjoyed and cherished. An explanation that people fall in and out of love is within the grasp of even very young children. Explaining that people can still like and love each other but not be able to live together helps. Many examples are available from television and within the child's own experience. She may have had a very special friend who she thought would be her best friend forever. When things changed and the friendship was not so attractive, then the friendship ended. However, it was not long before your child found another best friend.

During the book's introductory example a young boy asks his father, "Do you make love with the man you live with the same way you did with Mommy?" A seven-year-old boy likely had a concept of "making love" drawn from his experience of his mother and father always being together and being very special to each other. He probably is aware they engage in some behaviors he doesn't ask about, but for the most part he understands it is just a very special way loving adults have of sharing. After his father gave him an affirmative answer, the boy asked, "Isn't that against the law?"

His father answered, "Not anymore."

The boy replied, "Oh good. I wouldn't want you to get into trouble," and then the conversation moved on to other areas of interest, like what they were going to do on their next weekend visit.

Most school age children, of six to ten-years-old, understand words like "special kind of love." Many understand concepts like loving and wanting to be with a person of the same gender in the same way that Mommy and Daddy used to. At the same time, most children will not have a very active curiosity about what "loving someone else" entails. Suffice it to say: "We do special things together."

Ages ten to 12 and beyond are more complex times for children. They are beginning the long process of coming to grips with their own sexuality, as well as the onset of their own physical sexual maturity. They are becoming more overtly aware of things with a sexual connotation. Most likely they are becoming acquainted with the terms fag, queer, les, fruit, and many other slang phrases or words. I recently heard some ten to 12-year-old boys calling another "lips" as derogative homosexual innuendo. Remember your own experience at this age. Most of us had experiences of knowing someone in school who had the dreaded label of queer or fag. There may have been absolutely no knowledge of that person's sexuality. It was usually a boy who had some effeminate mannerisms, maybe slightly built and most frequently unpopular. His name may have been Bruce or Maurice. (Please forgive us, all the Bruces and Maurices. If you lived through it, you know the price. If you escaped it, you were fortunate.) We may have joined enmasse with the group persecuting B. for his famous "blow-jobs" without having the slightest idea what a "blow-job" was. This label cast him into the lowest, most sufferable position in the school's social hierarchy. Many children today of 12 and older have had exposure to gay roles, at least on television. This helps set the stage for more positive points of view other than those received at school or from playmates.

When telling your young children, you may ask if they know what certain words mean—words like fag, queer or whatever vernacular you may have heard locally. This should be done in a calm, sharing fashion with an open attitude. If your child has some idea of the meaning of these words, allow him to take the lead by defining the words as he understands them. It is helpful to share with him some of your childhood words, their uses and compare them with his. Keep in mind that he may have been one of the persecutors of the presumed gay schoolmate. This provides the opportunity to help him understand we all have a tendency at one time or another to go along with the crowd. Help him understand the important thing is being able to settle his own personal feelings in his heart. Many of us have had experiences with "enmasse psychology" ourselves at one time with some "different-ness." Perhaps sharing this with him may be beneficial, especially since that kind of behavior is often a natural part of growing up. Explain that another unfortunate thing that we do while growing up is the use of name calling as a way of enhancing our own self-esteem or saving face. Take this opportunity to coach him in more positive approaches to esteem building.

While coming out to your child, be aware that he could have been the victim of "enmasse" gay persecution in school. This may or may not be attributed to public knowledge of your sexuality. Nevertheless, it may present its own set of problems for him. Make sure the door is open if this happens to him.

Many different slang words and phrases are used to describe minority groups. It will be useful to your child's understanding of "different-ness" to provide your own more accurate and positive definitions, especially those describing gay and lesbian individuals. For early school age children, use words like "special love," "special attraction" or "special feeling" for another person of the same sex. Instead of using "same sex," you might use "another man or woman," since young children do not associate "sex" with Mommy and Daddy. Explain that because of these feelings, you and your partner (if you have one) have chosen to live together.

When sharing, be aware of your child's capacity to absorb new and perhaps difficult-to-understand information. Do not overload him with too much at once.

With open and caring attitudes about coming out, channels of communication should exist. Perhaps early during the coming out process, you could take some time to discuss the need for not sharing this information with everyone. Certainly there are some horror stories of a child innocently sharing this information at school only to find a social worker from the Department of Human Resources or Child Welfare knocking on the parent's door. Fortunately, this is the exception and not the rule.

References on keeping this a "family secret" should avoid analogies that infer shame (an alcoholic uncle or an unwed pregnant cousin) or disease (a crazy aunt or grandfather with cancer).[1] Comparing the situation to the time you were first considering divorce may be more on target. A premature announcement made publicly would have to be taken back if the divorce did not take place. Therefore the less said until things are final, the better.

Another reasonable analogy is the abortion issue. Each side thinks they are right, moral and just. Each has a sizeable backing to support their position. Some people feel this is a situation which strictly should be legislated and controlled, while others feel it is purely a matter of personal choice and responsibility. Because of the controversial nature of abortion, it may be more analogous to your homosexual experience. This is a good example of a "family secret" that is not shared with just anyone. Let him know who it is okay to tell.

This "family secret" is not a secret because anyone is ashamed of what has happened, or that it is wrong, but rather because some people will not agree. These people who do not agree may even have a tendency to speak out and try to cause trouble.

For more extensive examples of real-life situations, refer to the chapter on age-appropriate language.

---

[1]This example is not to imply that we feel there is anything shameful about alcoholism, out-of-wedlock pregnancy, having a mental or emotional disorder, or a natural disease process. But the prevailing social attitudes towards these examples is one your child is likely to understand. Take advantage of this opportunity to tell your child these are not things to be ashamed of or to tease about but that because of some people's poor understanding about them, they tactfully are kept a "family secret."

# The Risk of Telling

The question: "Won't my coming out cause my kids to suffer rejection, ridicule and emotional pain?" As mentioned earlier, with this question comes attitudes that transcend even the knowledge that homosexuality is an okay lifestyle; if a person is gay, that person is bad.

Unfortunately, the answer to the question may be yes and carries with it the same type of pain often experienced by children from families that are poor, interracial or which have a member who is slow to learn or disabled. Almost any variant in our society will suffer some rejection or even hostility. As long as there are people who see "different-ness" as always bad, those people will create pain for those affected.

We are, thankfully, living in a society of changing attitudes. It certainly was difficult in the early days of racial desegregation for black children who went to school under police escort. There were plenty of rough edges at first for those who had a neighbor of different color skin or who were friends with a "mixed race" child. Despite some ongoing problems with desegregation, in most areas of the country the difficult days of integration have now passed.

In much the same way, it may be difficult for your children to adjust to your coming out. But there will most

likely be less trauma than that which would have oc-
curred ten to 15 years ago. Working through some of
these difficulties now paves the way for an easier "integration" for children of gays ten to 15 years down the road,
just as the 1950's and 60's children did their part for racial integration we take for granted in the 1990's. It helps
to remember these adjustments are transient and will
pass provided your child is in a wholesome environment.
The importance of having an open, honest, warm, loving
and caring relationship—a full and lasting relationship
—with your child cannot be over emphasized. Sharing
that type of relationship with your children provides
needed strength and positive modeling that will enable
them to work through adjustments they will face in their
lifetimes.

Some children will say they wish you had never shared
this information with them, that the best thing you could
have done would be to have just gone away. Fortunately,
this situation occurs only occasionally, and even then
that attitude usually is more of a reflection of an inability
to adjust rather than a reaction based on real feelings.
This position will change if the door for a better relationship is left open. View this as an opportunity to help your
child learn to adjust to differences.

There is no guarantee that your children will make positive adjustments to your coming out. Some children do
not adjust. There will never be a close relationship
between them and their gay parents, just as there are distant relationships within many seemingly "intact" families. For a number of reasons, a close bond sometimes
never develops between the parent and child. This is an
opportunity for the parent to adjust to what is—the real
relationship—and continue to be available for a closer
bond should the circumstances change.

Some risks entail more than just short-term adjustment reactions to "different-ness." We touched on these
harsher reactions earlier in the book. We will more fully
explore them here.

There is a chance that coming out will result in severe negative reprisals. Some of these reprisals include changes in visitation (including supervised or severed visitation), loss of employment due to publicity, harassment from neighbors or other family members and the loss of custody.

An example of loss of custody happened several years ago in Dallas, Texas. In a much publicized case (Risher vs. Risher) Douglas—the non-gay father—was suing Mary Jo —the lesbian mother—for custody of their nine-year-old son, Richard. During the divorce, Mary Jo had been awarded custody of Richard and his teenage brother, Jimmy. Upon discovering she was lesbian and living with another lesbian mother—Ann and her daughter, Judy Ann—Douglas filed suit for a change in custody. There was abundant expert testimony regarding the fitness of the home, of Mary Jo and Ann as good mothers and of the home as being fit, safe, emotionally secure and favorable to Richard's normal development. Nevertheless, a transfer of custody was issued "in the best interest of the child, transferring him from a good home to a better home."[1]

A revised visitation suit, allowing only supervised visitation or in some cases no visitation at all, may be the result when your ex-spouse is not supportive of your coming out. In such cases, the argument often arises that the gay parent will in some way recruit the child into becoming homosexual or sexually molest the child (especially a child of the same sex), despite overwhelming evidence that sexual molestation of children is almost an exclusively heterosexual phenomenon.[2] As we've stated, there is further evidence that the incidence of homosexuality is no greater in children of gay or straight parents.

---

[1]*By Her Own Admission* (Gibson, Doubleday, New York 1977). This is a factual account taken from the transcripts of the trial and with the collaboration of Mary Jo Risher.

[2]90% of molestation cases are heterosexual, usually involving the father, step-father, uncle or another male well known to the child.

Recent court decisions have upheld grandparents' rights to sue for custody of minor grandchildren despite the wishes of their custodial birth parent. Even parties other than the non-gay parent—an aunt or uncle or an older brother or sister—may bring legal pressure to bear if they are non-supportive of gay lifestyles.

This news is not intended to frighten you or dissuade you from coming out to your children. Keep in mind that although these cases receive a lot of publicity, these unfortunate outcomes are rare. We would be remiss in our duty, however, if we led you to believe that coming out is not without potential pitfalls. Here again are more examples of reasons to establish a positive support group around you. Seek legal counsel before sharing if you feel any disastrous results might occur. Find out if there is a chapter of Gay Parents in your area, so you can hear an exchange of experiences from a wider variety of situations. Coming out is an important experience—one which will benefit you and your children, especially if you plan well and make good use of your support systems.

# Your Partner...Who Is (S)he to Your Child?

I f you have a partner or are looking for one, a lot of consideration should be given to who this person is to your child.

The ideal situation would be one in which your new partner takes on the role of a surrogate parent, sharing duties, powers and responsibilities with you and adding one more positive model to those roles already filled by you and your ex-spouse.

Here is an example of the least desired situation: John is the custodial parent of his son, Matt. Dick, John's lover, is unsure of his parenting role. Because of John's uncertainty about his parenting role, Matt is equally confused. During times when Dick and John are getting along well, Matt experiences Dick as a surrogate parent as described above. During times when John and Dick are not getting along well, Matt experiences Dick as a somewhat unwelcome boarder who is forbidden to discipline, exercise authority over or in any way relate to him. In this example, Matt becomes a power pawn between John and Dick, tossed about freely while they fight, thus creating serious role-confusion for him.

This last example is not exclusive to gay relationships. Precisely this same scenario frequently occurs in straight relationships, where there has been a divorce and now a step or adoptive-parent has emerged. When the parents are getting along fine, so go the parenting roles. When occasional trouble arises, the natural parent becomes the only parent. The step or adoptive parent becomes an unwelcome intruder.

These last two situations obviously provide the grounds on which to play sometimes vicious power games, usually detrimental to your relationship and your child.

Risking redundancy we reiterate: we do not live in a perfect world. There are few, if any, "Leave It to Beaver" or "Ozzie and Harriet" families. We have no quarrel with the wholesome quality of family life or the smoothness of operation demonstrated in those television shows. However, most families do not operate that smoothly. We are suggesting possibilities for your situation. Even though these may not be ideal for every circumstance we trust they will provide a place to start.

The first and perhaps most important step is to find out from your partner and children how they want to experience their respective roles. The younger your children, the less likely it is they will have much concern in this area. Older children may well want to form more of a friendship or an aunt/uncle type relationship with your partner. Given that your partner does want some degree of a parenting role, there should be some discussion and agreement about how this role can be accomplished. It is beneficial to have similar values and ideas on role modeling, discipline and parenting responsibilities. Please note that in the absence of adoption by the non-parent partner (which would not be legal anyway if the parents are of the same sex), legal considerations and responsibilities belong first to the natural custodial parent, then the non-custodial parent, then—with special arrangements—the partner. Refer to the chapter on legal considerations for general guidelines. For specific advice consult your personal attorney.

Several relationship situations might develop. Each needs considerable thought if children, natural or adoptive, are to be brought into your relationship.

**Situation 1.** This relationship includes Mary and Jane who want to parent and be as equal as possible in their co-parenting roles. One or both partners may be birth parents from previous heterosexual relationships, or one or both may wish to undergo adoption proceedings in order to become an adoptive parent (most states now have statutes allowing for single parent adoption). In this relationship Mary is the parent. She and Jane agree that their parenting duties and obligations take on a very high priority for both even though Mary is the legal parent. Mary and Jane provide a united parenting partnership, agree to settle together the issues of rewards, discipline, rules, family attitudes, privileges, duties and the like. It is especially important in this situation that Jane be presented to Bev (Mary's child) as filling a parent role, with all the authority and responsibility that goes with the job. Jane has no binding legal charge over Bev unless certain limited special arrangements are made, but the effect of her responsibilities remains the same. This type of relationship and co-parenting situation works best with younger children since they are more pliable to parenting situations and to parent figures.

Jane is encouraged to assist Bev in understanding that her role is not to take the place of Mike, Bev's father, but rather to serve as an additional or "helping" parent. We recommend that every effort be made to reinforce the integrity of the non-custodial mother or father. In the case of adoption, we also encourage reinforcing the integrity of birth parents, even though little if any information may be available about them.

If older children are involved, they should be included in the role decision for the non-parent partner to the extent they are comfortable and capable. Older children may prefer and be more comfortable with an aunt, uncle or friend type of relationship, as opposed to trying to develop an acceptance of the non-parent partner as a parent figure. This model is also adaptive to situations in which the gay parent is the non-custodial parent, has good visitation rights and a good supportive relationship with the custodial parent.

**Situation 2.** This relationship includes John, who is the natural, adoptive or otherwise primary parent, and Dick, who is unsure of the role for himself for any number of reasons. In this situation, where the parenting role for Dick is more optional, John and Dick are encouraged to discuss at length Dick's assumption of his role as a parent and the accompanying duties and responsibilities. There will be a major impact on their relationship and it should be explored beforehand, to determine if the results will be beneficial or detrimental to their relationship and John's child. Dick may want to read some literature on parenting or visit a Gay/Lesbian Parents Group to discuss the role of non-parent partners.

We are aware there will be situations in which a natural parent cannot postpone assuming full parenting responsibilities, such as would be the case if the other natural parent suddenly died or abandoned her child. In that case it would be natural to expect the parent partner to immediately assume his role and responsibility for his child; those responsibilities did not become optional during the custody hearing. Expecting this emergent situation, this type of partnership can enjoy the luxury of time while making parenting decisions. This kind of preparation is encouraged of any couple planning a family.

In this situation the non-parent partner, after due consideration, may opt for a co-parenting role such as described in Situation 1. He may choose a modified role, more like an uncle, deferring all major decisions for child rearing to the primary parent. This latter example is frequently found in relationships where there is the natural parent and a step or non-adoptive parent in heterosexual divorce/second marriage situations.

**Situation 3.** This relationship includes Jane, who is a natural or adoptive or potentially adoptive parent, or one who desires to parent through a surrogate mother. Mary is an individual who has no desire whatsoever to be—or even consider being—a parent, or to be put into a parenting role.

In this case, very careful consideration needs to be given to the relationship and the assumption of a parenting role by Jane. We encourage Jane and Mary to discuss and explore their relationship and individual life goals to determine if they are mutually compatible. Careful consideration should be given to the continuation of this relationship. Jane should understand that any child brought into this relationship would possibly be experienced as an intruder in Mary's time and space—a competitor for attention and affections. Mary and the child could become rivals.

If Mary and Jane's child become rivals, both Jane and Mary need to consider this point: the child (especially as an infant) had little if anything to say about being born or coming into the relationship. In that sense, the child should not be expected to compete for love, affection and attention, as these should be the inherent rights of any child.

In a situation where there is an impasse between Mary and Jane about wanting vs. not wanting children, we would encourage giving realistic consideration to dissolving the relationship with each person seeking out a partner whose goals and aspirations regarding the parenting issue are more compatible with her own. In this case, neither partner is right or wrong. The needs and goals of the partners are just different and most likely cannot be realized in the same relationship.

While being a parent lasts a lifetime, the very active phase of parenting last only a few years. It is these few years that are the most important in your child's lifetime, as they lay the foundation on which he builds his experiences. Parenting, therefore, should not be entered into without careful thought and consideration for all parties involved.

# How Do I Know
# If This Is Detrimental
# to My Child?

**B**efore getting involved in an indepth discussion of whether or not this sharing could be detrimental to your child, we should look at the adjustment reactions that occur with most major changes. Change frequently is associated with pain, just as it frequently is accompanied by excitement and expectancy.

A major change like divorce or coming out and sharing information about a lifestyle that may be alien or at least misrepresented to your child, is similar to the grief changes that accompany the loss of a loved one.

At the earliest recognition that there has been or is going to be loss, there is the tendency to deny that it is happening. A general behavior is to continue the status quo as if there was no change or loss. Any attempt to discuss the loss is met with resistance, avoidance, retreat or outright denial.

After a period of time when the loss or change, actual or impending, is blatantly obvious, there is a tendency to try to negotiate the change. This is a time of bargaining when the agreement becomes "I'll do anything to make this change less or not at all."

As time passes and the consequences of the change must be lived with, there is a tendency to become angry at the change, whether that be a concept (like a relationship) or an actual person (like the now absent parent).

Soon, however, it becomes obvious that neither denial, bargaining, nor anger will change the course of events. At this point the tendency is to become pensive and depressed while adjusting. This behavior opens the way for acceptance, it makes the event real to the person and in turn allows it to become a part of his experiences and relationships.

The final stage of adjusting to change is acceptance. This is acceptance of "the way it is" and, in all likelihood, the way things will remain. It is during this phase of processing change that the person becomes available again to bond with those who are around him.

All of these stages are healthy and should be encouraged. These stages are neither isolated nor mutually exclusive to one another. A person may vacillate between stages, skip a stage only to come back and work through it later or may fuse several stages at once. The hallmark of successful resolution is arriving at the acceptance phase. There is no accurate time table for any person. It is safe to assume that a few weeks to months would be a rapid resolution. However, resolving loss and change is very individual, and each person should be given adequate time to work through the stages in his own manner. However, if one gets caught up in the early stages of denial, bargaining or anger, there may be cause for concern. If there is a prolonged depressive phase, we encourage you to seek professional help in achieving resolution for the person stuck in non-acceptance.

We should point out that acceptance is different than approval. Acceptance is the acknowledgment of the state of things—in this case a divorce has taken place, a parent is gay. The reaction that comes with acceptance may be either approval or disapproval.

Here are some signs or behaviors indicating that your child may be having a difficult and negative reaction to your coming out, and that some intervention may be required.

Most of us have some reaction to major change. Most of these reactions are due to what we learned from past experiences. These reactions usually resolve themselves over time in an atmosphere of patience, guidance and understanding, but sometimes they do not; it can be difficult to distinguish short-term, reactive behavior from serious, lasting troubles.

For example, a six-year-old boy undergoing the rigors of his parents' divorce begins regressive behaviors of bedwetting, having to sleep with the light on, talking baby talk and carrying a blanket.

This same behavior had been seen in his sister two years prior when the family moved, uprooting her from school and classmates, when she was at the age of seven. The behavior lasted a few weeks and she returned to her age-appropriate seven-year-old behaviors.

Thinking that the boy would likewise return to age-appropriate behaviors, his parents tolerated the situation and postponed the divorce. After six months without change, his parents decided to proceed with the divorce. Now almost seven, he intentionally began to soil his pants. It was then that intervention was sought.

While this kind of behavior in the daughter was transient and no cause for great concern, in the boy it was long-term and problematic, and the remedy took several months of professional intervention.

The best guide as to whether your child's behaviors are short-lived, self-limiting and non-problematic, or symptoms of a more serious adjustment problem, is your child's previous history. A sudden loss of interest in school or a drop in grades in an otherwise good student can be an early warning. A placid child suddenly acting out with friends with unusual aggression or trying to start fights may alert friends and teachers to a problem. Regression to younger or even infantile behavior, if lasting more than a few days, can be the signs of a deeply troubled child. Sleep disturbances or a major variation of eating habits may be present with or without symptoms. Social withdrawal and isolation by an otherwise outgoing child are indications that there is something going on emotionally which needs investigation. This unexplained behavior may or may not be because you are gay and have come out. Nonetheless, it does mean something is wrong and early intervention can prevent further complications and problems,.

Depending on your child's age, intervention may mean using an analogy with which he can identify. Personalizing the analogy makes it safer for him to own his feelings: "I remember when I was about your age and my best friend who lived next door told me his parents were getting a divorce. I knew enough about divorce to know a child can't live with both parents at the same time, so I asked him who he was going to live with. At the time he didn't know, but he thought he was going to live with his mother. This worried him because he heard Mom say it was okay for Dad to keep the house because she wanted to move as far away as possible. It didn't take me long to figure out that my friend would be moving, so I got very scared. I started to ignore my friend, wouldn't talk or play with him, and once even tried to start a fight. I thought my feelings were strange, because while I had these angry feelings, my friendship feelings were still there. It was only after talking about those feelings with my Mom and Dad that I discovered that I could still see my friend, they were only moving across town. I also discovered these feelings were normal feelings and that Mom and Dad had experienced similar feelings. My friendship did change some and I found another best friend who lived close by, but my first friend and I continued to be friends and see each other. In fact, we are still friends today."

With older children, intervention may be made more direct by asking your child outright if he has some bothersome feelings about your being gay. While doing this we encourage you to provide an atmosphere that is supportive where their feelings are respected.

Finding out the nature of the problem with children can be difficult and complicated at best. Just asking, "What's the problem?" invokes images of someone in trouble. There may be special fears on your child's part; since the problem is "you," they are making a judgment on someone they love. Therefore, it may be up to you to let your child know it is okay to have the reactions he is having. If that reaction is problematic, the invitation is present to work through these difficult feelings. Give permission by saying, "It is okay to feel guilt or uneasy about something that is different. It is okay even if that is about me being gay." The goal then becomes to give enough helpful and healthy information about being gay to get through those problematic feelings.

Indications that your child is having trouble might present themselves within the relationship you have with your partner. Frequently the child will try to sabotage the relationship in the hope that things will return to "how it used to be." This type of sabotage does not happen just where the parent happens to be gay. Many divorced/ remarried couples, where there is a step-parent, experience children from one marriage pitting parent against step-parent. Since this behavior is done more out of manipulation than malevolence, caretaking concern is in order when trying to intervene in your child's sabotage. Help your child understand that changes do occur and will occur during his lifetime. Adjusting to those changes, even if painful, is necessary and a part of life and growing up.

The previously mentioned signs of maladjustment will certainly be obvious to you if you are the custodial parent. If you are not the custodial parent, and you and your partner still share responsibility for some child rearing, take time to discuss these changes with him.

This type of upfront responsibility will provide good modeling for your child in coping with life changes. It will promote open communication for your children regarding changes during life and differences among people.

# The Adoptive
# Gay Parent

We are living in an era of dramatic changes in the structure of family, marriage, bonding and child rearing. While the mother/father or husband/wife structures remain the basis for the majority of nuclear families, we are seeing many more non-married cohabiting families, single parents and now surrogate parenting. With some of these dramatic changes we are seeing more and more gay men and lesbian women wanting to be parents. It goes without saying that many gays already are parents from current or previous heterosexual unions—this is the primary subject of this book. Being gay does not exclude you from the ability, nor the desire, to be parents.

On the other hand, there are those gays who have chosen not to complicate matters by getting involved in a heterosexual union, knowing beforehand that such a relationship would not work. Such realization does not extinguish the desire for parenthood, so many gays and lesbians have resorted to single-parent adoption. Because this is legal in most states, the occurrence of single-parent adoptions has become rather commonplace. Contrary to popular belief, gays can and do adopt children, from infants to teens. Depending on where you live, local sentiment will dictate the ease or difficulty you encounter during the adoption process. There are certainly parts of the country in which adoption would be denied if your homosexuality were to be exposed. There are other areas where adoption is based on the demonstration of a person's desire and ability to parent, not his or her sexuality. There are even some areas in which efforts are made to foster or adopt out "identified pre-gay" or gay children (usually teens) to gay parents, although we have never been sure of the exact criteria for the determination of "identified pre-gay."

The argument has been and will continue to be made that if a person wants to be a parent he or she should get married and "do it right." But it is simply a reality that gay and lesbian parents do exist and will continue to exist. Some previously have been married, others opt for single parent adoption. Women who can conceive can arrange for artificial insemination. Both men and women can utilize the services of a surrogate who will bear a child for them. We must address the issue that concerns them in a healthy, holistic fashion, if for no other reason than to benefit the children of these parents.

Unlike many children born to couples, a child born to artificially inseminated women or surrogate mothers usually is well planned for and fairly well assured of having a home with love and care. The same goes for the child adopted through routine channels. Chances are these children of gay or lesbian parents have been planned for and eagerly anticipated over a period of years.

It is in this very plan that you may face, multifaceted problems as well as boundless joys. If you have cultivated a good support system, this "selective parenting" will be accepted and supported. If you provide a wealth of loving emotions for your selected child, the going and growing for her should be fairly easy.

When you come out to your child, she may hit you with the question, "Why did you have me in the first place if you thought it was going to be tough for me?" It may seem to your child that you chose to dump some of your difficulty on her head without her having a vote.

In our experience it is not unusual to have a child be-moan the fact she has interracial, disabled, single, poor or old parents. When we get right down to it, the question is not at all that unusual for any child to ask, especially in times of stress or during those years when it is so difficult to be different or part of a difference. She usually will work through this stage as long as there is an atmosphere of love, understanding and acceptance.

We encourage the adoptive gay parent, like any other adoptive parent, to assure your adopted child she was chosen with careful thought and planning. Let your child know she was given every consideration possible. Make it clear you chose this parenting role with full knowledge there would be special problems to be man-aged and worked through. However, you choose to view these problems more as challenges and that every time each of you meets another challenge, you grow one more notch. With that attitude each new generation of children of gays will have an easier time. Acknowledge that as un-derstanding and acceptance by the rest of society grows, books such as this will become merely references as to how it was in "the old days."

# Whose Pain
# Is It Anyway?

In previous chapters we mentioned the client who told us he was afraid of hurting his parents, friends or children by revealing his homosexuality. While respecting anyone who wants to spare another pain, we question the true motive behind not telling. In attempting to promote high-level wellness in gays, we always strive to diminish the internal response that says "gay is bad" and that coming out must cause pain in others. We frequently ask, "Whose pain are you really protecting?" It is difficult to forecast another person's reaction to hearing that a friend, family member or parent is gay. We have had experiences with friends from supposedly very open, caring and loving support groups who were completely ostracized after coming out. Conversely, we have had friends whose support group was mainly of a judgmental conservative, religious mindset who welcomed the information openly and lovingly. Children are equally unpredictable, each case being unique to the situation in that particular family.

As we get into the pain of the information, we should be mindful of the coming out process. For most of us it was, or perhaps still is, a long and arduous task, full of uncertainty, disappointment, guilt, tears and soul searching.

There is the fear, and sometimes the reality, that if you come out, you might be disowned by your family. Sometimes there is the angry response that being gay has to be someone else's fault. Usually targeted in that fault-finding search are our parents or perhaps the lack of parents. Sometimes it was a divorce or remarriage, that seemed to be at fault. The list could go on indefinitely. Yet in reality, there is no fault, no place to lay the blame for being gay. As we are well aware now, there is no causal factor in being or becoming gay. Being gay is a normally occurring variant in the human population.[1]

If we have an overriding fear that coming out will necessarily cause pain in someone else, then that is an indication that we need more self-acceptance work. We are not saying that no one with whom you share this information will experience pain; many people will, especially if this comes as a total surprise. However, we should divide pain into two types. One is a reactive pain similar to that experienced when we are informed that a loved one has had a heart attack or died. The news is sudden and unexpected. This is a real event that wishing and circumstances cannot change. It is not accompanied by a sense of shame or of being less than whole when shared. It is an experiential pain that we react and adjust to and then continue living as complete a life as possible.

Another kind of pain we feel, while reactive, may be more lasting. Frequently we also feel a sense of shame and of being less than whole. This pain usually accompanies news that a loved one or a family member has committed a crime-like robbery or murder and now must pay the penalty. The person committing the crime will be around for years to come and he is still family or friend. His very being reminds the family of the shameful act and in that sense the pain is ongoing.

Both types of pain can be experienced by different gays and their families. Increasingly, more gays and their fam-

---

[1] Using an updated version of the Kinsey report and Weinberg and Bell's studies, the human population has always had ± 10% homosexuals as a part of the total population regardless of societal support or condemnation during different eras.

ilies experience the former—reactive/adjustment type of pain—rather than the latter—criminal/lasting shame sort of pain. Our experience will largely be a matter of self-esteem, background and attitude.

Earlier we included a note written by a client. ". . . because telling that you are gay has to be kept secret, it's something to feel guilty about. At this point, it's almost a sense of keeping one's integrity not to tell, but it's such a part of our total existence, our total experience, our total selves. I am so aware of the singularity of my existence, having to live this way. It's very bothersome. The craziness of having to have a secret life when you have no desire to be secretive, and in that very essence, guilt thrives. If you can't tell something, it must be bad, that feeling you know . . ." In a sense, the author of that note was still struggling with his shame, pain and guilt that frequently accompanies coming out. During this phase the thought of sharing often brings on a sense of inferiority. It also is during these times that we have an immature or less complete self-image than we actually are. It is sometimes compared to feeling as if we were a teenager, seeking parental approval while wanting to begin our own independent life.

This loss of approval—the threat of being seen by loved ones as less than whole, or not as complete as our straight brother or sister—frequently accompanies the fear of having love withdrawn. This fear causes a massive amount of internal pain. It is this very unpleasant pain that we live with for such a very long period of time. It is frequently projected onto people we love and to whom we are going to come out. There is every reason to respect not wanting to create that type of pain in our loved ones, but we must keep in mind, that *fear is a projection of our pain.* It is not necessarily going to be and usually is not their experience. We cannot know their internal experience. We can know only our own and the more painful it is, the more threatening coming out will be. Nevertheless, we must realize that it is our pain and we must work through it. The projection that we will hurt them may also rob them of a more complete and real relationship with us. Please keep in mind, just as we had—or are still having—our coming out experience to deal with, our loved ones, be they parents, friends or children, will also have theirs. If we are nevertheless telling ourselves at this moment that coming out to our loved ones will cause them pain, we may be correct. In the majority of cases, this will be reactive/adjustment pain that they will work through. A quality relationship will surface that is at least as good as or better than the one prior to coming out. Frequently, the quality of relationship is far superior after coming out.

If, on the other hand, we are telling ourselves this information will kill our loved ones, that they will never work through it, that they will disown us, etc., we probably are projecting our own pain onto them. We freely admit that some people do experience very poor results after telling. However, this is the exception and not the rule.[2]

Similarly, if we are telling ourselves "if they (the loved ones) wanted to know, they'd ask," we may be fooling ourselves. Sometimes we operate under the delusion that everyone already knows but no one talks about it. If this truly is the case, we probably want to come out but are hoping someone else will set the stage by asking questions. By so doing, they assume our responsibility for starting the coming out process. Under any circumstances we feel this is a responsibility that should be borne by us. When it comes to telling your child (children), it is even more imperative that this be your responsibility. As we mentioned earlier, this could be an awesome responsibility for your child to shoulder. Depending on his age, your child may (will) have a difficult time sorting through myth vs. fact, rumor vs. experience. Your child may have many of the same fears as you, in that he

---

[2]In polling area psychotherapists, *The Dallas Morning News* reported surprisingly similar results: 90-95% of all coming out cases were successful with very positive results.

may fear loss of love or retaliation if he ventures to share a hidden and protected part of your life.

Sometimes that responsibility is thrust upon your child. Several years ago you may have seen the television movie, *That Certain Summer.* In that story a son, visiting the home of his gay father and male lover, finds his father's watch with a revealing love inscription from his lover. In that situation, as a young teen, the son had many questions and virtually no one to turn to; therefore he had to find an indirect way (running away) to force the issue to the surface.

We know of one case in which two male partners had the son and daughter of one of the partners in their home for a weekend visit. The children, being too young to pay caution to curiosity, were looking for a videotape movie to entertain themselves. They knew Daddy was supposed to get some movies for them to watch; while searching for *Superman* or *Star Wars,* they came across adult-type male/male video and unwittingly were exposed to explicit male/male sexual activity. This created a lot of unnecessary confusion at an early age. The same scenario has happened with sexually explicit and not-so-explicit gay-oriented literature. Needless to say, when the children presented this information and set of accompanying questions to their mother, more than just coming out was at hand.

Similarly, in the case of a lesbian couple, both mothers of several children, each had chosen not to come out to their children. In this situation, some of the children were grown, some were teens and others were pre-teens. One of the older girls found non-sexual lesbian-oriented literature. This material dealt with positive lesbian lifestyles and living. The books were along the lines of Berzon's *Positively Gay* or Weinberg's *Society and the Healthy Homosexual.* When the daughter found the book she was outraged, not so much because Mom was lesbian but because she felt their relationship had been a lie. She recounted all of her unanswered questions— about the divorce, living with this other woman and her children, and the hidden private lives the two mothers had assumed—all the while she had never felt a comfortable environment in which to seek information that would explain their behavior.

In these situations, the parents had not come out in order to avoid handling their own pain. All admitted wanting an easy way out, stating something like: "It would be easier if someone would just ask." All experienced some degree of relief at the discovery or being gay or lesbian even though it brought on multiple issues to be handled in a time of crisis.

In writing this chapter, we are not under the illusion that sharing facts about being gay will be free of pain. After all, the self-discovery that we are gay is frequently accompanied by pain. The coming out process is usually long, hard, soul searching and full of pain and questions. Coming to terms with our own sexuality and how that will influence us and our relationships also is trying and painful. We must make peace with ourselves that being gay is part of our life, for whatever reason. The pain generated by this fact is our pain, despite its many sources over which we have little control. The responsibility to share this information with your support group—part of whom is your children—is yours. The manner in which you take on that responsibility of sharing will in great measure determine the long-term relationship with your children. Rest assured that in our experience, in that of other therapists and in the experience of hundreds of gay and lesbian individuals we know personally, the pain is reactive and relatively short-term. The outcome is well worth the risk.

# Preparing to Share

**H**ere is the moment this book has been preparing you for: The event and experience of sharing with your children that you are gay or lesbian.

Before sharing with your children, we encourage you to discuss your intentions with one or more people you know and trust. Most certainly this would include your partner, if you have one. We especially encourage your consulting your partner, not to seek permission (for the decision should be yours), but rather for preparation and support. You also might need someone as a sounding board after you've talked with your child. If there are difficult moments, your partner, friends or family can support you in working through them. If there is only acceptance and understanding, you'll have someone to share your joy. Most likely, you can expect some combination of positive and negative reactions.

When choosing a time for the share, pick a time that is relatively stress free. This sharing should not be done during or just after the divorce, a major move or any other major situational stresses you or your children may be experiencing. Choose a private place and time when no one's schedule is rushed. Unplug the phone so there are no interruptions.

Early in the discussion, reassure your child. Let him know this talk is not disciplinary in nature, nothing is wrong. Give your child plenty of permission, time and latitude to ask any questions that come up for him.

As we've said, very young children should receive a rather sketchy, simplistic explanation. Their questions, if any, will most probably be equally simplistic in nature. For example your child might ask, "Does that mean Mommie will not live with us any more?" or "Will I have another Daddy now?"

The older the child, the fuller an explanation will be called for. Most likely, more complex questions will be asked by an older child, too. Some older children will want to reflect and then ask questions later. These requests should be granted. Children of all ages should be assisted in understanding that coming out is an ongoing process and the door always is open for a more complete and better understanding.

The degree of support from spouse, ex-spouse and other outside parties will in large measure suggest the degree to which coming out must be kept a "family secret."

Allow for plenty of time. As we previously mentioned, this is an ongoing process with this initial share being only the first step in the process. Support your child in having his own experience and feelings regarding coming out. Reassure them that your love and acceptance is NOT based on their response to you. It is important for them to feel your love for them is intact, standing above anything that should happen during or after coming out.

We encourage you to be supportive of your ex-spouse, whether he or she is supportive or not in return. This book is about building and strengthening relationships and about having real relationships. Keep in mind your child's right to have as intact and positive a relationship with both parents as is possible under the circumstances. This right should (MUST) be preserved and respected. Frequently the rights of the child are abbreviated or altogether terminated because of conflicts between the embattled spouses, who have become more interested in their vindictiveness and reprisals against each other than interested in the welfare of their child.

The less your child knows about your lifestyle prior to coming out, the more reactive he will likely be. However, we have clients who caught their children by surprise with the information only to discover that their children readily accept and adjust and go on about their routines as if coming out made little difference. In fact, we have had a number of clients whose children actually helped them—the parents—make the transition of coming out by saying, "Oh, come on, Dad. Get with it. We know you are gay. Come out of the closet and enjoy life."

Depending on your child's background and age, he may have some religious-oriented questions for you. Since this is such a personal area, we feel it is best to not get into this aspect in this book. Seek personal counsel with your pastor or one of the pastors of a church with a special outreach to the gay and lesbian community, like one of the numerous Metropolitan Community Churches. However, we do feel we can be of some service in this area by supplying you with a list of selected references that may assist you in preparing for and answering those religious questions: *The Church and the Homosexual* by McNeil, *Is the Homosexual My Neighbor* by Scanzoni and Mollenkott, *But Lord, They're Gay* by Pennington, and *The Lord Is My Shepherd and He Knows I'm Gay* by Perry. This list is by no means exhaustive or complete. Any one of these books will provide some religious insights that may prove helpful and will provide resources and materials addressing homosexuality and religion.

Depending on how detailed your coming out is going to be (which will be mostly dictated by the age and maturity of your child), you may choose to rehearse this with someone else. Seek out someone who already has had this experience and share any questions or concerns you may have. Keep in mind, whether that individual's experience was positive or negative, it was their's and not yours. This person is only a sounding board and not a decision maker for you.

Review the chapter on age-appropriate language and analogies to prepare for your particular situation. We have included examples from people who have already experienced coming out to their children covering a wide range of ages and custodial issues.

Keep in mind there will most likely be a difference in how and what you tell and when (regarding your child's age) you tell depending on whether or not you have custody and if your ex-spouse is supportive or not. We can only reflect that if you do not have custody and your ex-spouse is supportive, there will be little difference between your situation and that of the gay or lesbian parent who has custody. In cases of non-support or hostility between the parents, we encourage you to weigh potential risk and complications carefully, seek support and discuss this with counsel, especially your divorce attorney and a counselor trained in this area.

Whatever your decision, good luck in your relationships. Now let's turn to some examples of language and analogies used in real situations depending on age and custody arrangements.

# Age-Appropriate Language

This chapter on age-appropriate language, analogies and metaphors is designed to be used as a guide only. Children mature at different speeds, some faster and others slower. Therefore, your child may be psychologically ahead or behind his chronological age.

Our best advice to you is to compare your child's behavior and interests to other children of his own age. If your child appears to behave, use language and have interests similar to his agemates, he is probably typical for that age and your analogies and language use should be designed for that age group. If on the other hand your child behaves and uses language like children much younger or older than his chronological age, tailor your language and analogies for the appropriate adjusted age group.

Please keep in mind that this chapter is only a guide. It cannot answer all of the questions your child may have nor can it cover all the information your child wants to know. No one knows your child better than you. Trust your own intuition and knowledge of your child. Also talk to your support group and glean ideas from them. Use them as a sounding board to practice the first of many talks regarding coming out as a gay person that you will have with your child. If you have older children who already know you are gay, or if you have gay friends with children to whom they have come out, use them as a valuable resource. Ask them about timing, language, and examples used in their experiences and how this affected them.

Since many gay and lesbian parents are natural parents and more gays and lesbians are adopting infants or using surrogates, we will start with modeling behavior to a child who is not old enough to speak or convey his level of understanding to you.

There is no age too young to witness and experience a warm, close, caring and loving relationship. This is true for your relationship between you and your partner and equally important between you and your child.

Up to the age of one (and in fact throughout your child's life), do not be afraid to show appropriate affection to your partner (if you have one) and your friends. Your best guide to "appropriate affection" is that which you see modeled by other parents to their children. Encourage a bonding relationship between your child and your partner as the additional parent figure. Begin to establish a reference name for your partner, so early on a kinship will begin to develop between him and your child. Since your partner will take on a significant role in your child's life, it is important to establish an early trust bond that will enhance your child's sense of security and belonging to the "family unit."

For all ages we discourage the use of terms like "other mother/father" to identify your partner. Instead we encourage affectional terms like "Nanna," which one of our clients used for her partner, after adopting an infant. Most parents and parent surrogates prefer names that convey a kindred bond without creating role confusion for the child. However, we can conceive of no problem in using your partner's own name when making reference about him to your child. If your affectional relationship is apparent to your child during this young age, the more complex sharing about being gay will happen much easier.

We are aware the majority of people reading this book will not have the opportunity to come out to their child at this early age. Most parents—gay, lesbian or straight—will handle this matter when the child is older. During the ages of early language development and increased capacity to understand (one to three years) it is doubtful your child will be able to conceptualize the significance of relationships.

During this time and even earlier, children learn to recognize the difference between mother and father and that between mother and other females as well as between father and other males. Soon they can distinguish aunts, uncles, grandparents and begin to associate the name with the person. However, this is still early for your child to grasp a concept as complex as a relationship. We continue to encourage your coming out to be a combination of modeling appropriate affectional behavior with your partner and friends as well as whatever affectional terms you and your partner share with one another. This is where your child will begin the subconscious process of identifying your partner and/or support group as being significant to you. Much more emphasis is placed on your partner, if you have one, since your child will associate terms of endearment with the same terms used by other couples for their partners and loved ones. Although your child will probably still fall short of fully conceptualizing the relationship, the association as to the significance of the other person will begin to develop.

As your child enters the age of four to six you can begin to add more of the building blocks that will aid in understanding you, your lifestyle and relationship.

It is during this age your child may begin to ask questions regarding his other parent, why you do not live together, or in the case of adoption, why the other parent is absent. Since the examples involving these ages and older get rather involved, we will present the case histories that outline real experiences for specific age groups.

Keep in mind the coming out process is long and frequently slow. Likewise the acceptance phase of your coming out is gradual and progressive. Remember, you did not come out to yourself or others overnight. Your children will not totally accept or understand your gay behavior overnight. We encourage you to be patient with the process you and your children are going through.

We realize that when reading the following cases, it appears as if one or two meetings were held between the parents and children, and "zappo," instant acceptance. Not true. These accounts are condensed versions of complex and lengthy periods of sharing and growing together. Most of them evolved over several months to a few years.

The following accounts are real life situations. The identifying characteristics have been changed to protect the integrity and privacy of the clients involved in these situations.

**Case Study**    Our book began with an unexpected question that forced the issue of coming out. "Daddy, do you make love with the man you live with the way you and Mommy did?" This was a situation in which the father had planned to come out to his son one day, but not this soon. Not that much time had passed since the divorce. His son, who we will call Lawrence was only seven at the time; the father, who we will call James, felt his son was going through enough at the time.

James had suggested during the course of his therapy that we set aside some time to discuss his gay issues and how to approach his son with them. Lawrence was a bright and intuitive boy. There was little doubt in my mind that he would figure out what was going on. However, during the course of the separation and divorce, Lawrence had begun some regressive behaviors. He began to carry James' shirt around and use occasional baby talk. He frequently asked James senseless questions in order to keep him on the phone. During home visits, Lawrence would be distant to James during the first part of the weekend and very clinging on Sunday afternoon, just prior to his departure.

It was while trying to intervene in this behavior that Lawrence asked the question.

James was surprised by the nature of the question, but had decided that no matter how coming out happened, he was going to be truthful from the first word.

Therefore James said yes to the question and thereby started the coming out process.

There were several things in James' life that complicated this process. He was a member of a very conservative, fundamentalist religion. Not only did this religion frown severely on divorce, but also it found homosexuality totally unacceptable. His ex-wife was threatening to deny any visitation because of the gay issue. He had wanted to share this issue with his son, but preferred his ex-wife to have a greater acceptance and understanding first, if possible. Unfortunately, Lawrence's timing did not allow that, so James had to handle the situation as it developed.

Although Lawrence was only seven, he evidently knew enough about relationships to use terms like "make love." James matched his son's terms and used the same level of communication replying, "Yes, son, I do." Then Lawrence went on to ask: "Isn't that against the law?" James responded, "No, not any more." Sounding relieved, Lawrence said, "Oh good, I wouldn't want you to get into trouble!"

This is a good example of answering only what is asked and meeting Lawrence at his model of the world. Lawrence had a specific issue in mind—was his father going to get in trouble with the law? After those concerns were settled, Lawrence did not ask any questions regarding the gay situation for a number of months.

This type of response is good especially if they are the ones who introduce the subject first. We have experienced examples where the parent was afraid to admit being gay to their children when asked equally innocent questions. While taking care of their own discomfort, they would respond with answers like . . . "What do you mean making love?" . . . or worse yet, scold the child for using such terms as "making love" or "sleeping with someone." In an effort to put up a smoke screen around talking about being gay, many parents confuse their children by giving them extraneous information to deal with instead of finding out what they want to know.

We indeed encourage you to find out what your children

want to know, but not take them on an information chase. Much of your communication will be affected by your vocal tone and volume and body language as well as what you say. Sometime how something is said is what gets interpreted rather than what is said.

It is not our intent here to criticize parents who have fallen into this trap. Our most sincere intent is to model a better method of coming to terms with how your being gay effects your relationship with your children.

**Case Study**     Think for a moment how Lawrence might have responded to an angry tone of voice with an answer like "What do you mean, making love," or "where did you ever hear a word like that, shame on you." This could have had devastating effects on Lawrence, especially in light of the fact he only wanted to know if his father was going to get into trouble for a behavior which he did not fully understand yet. Since Lawrence did not inquire more about James' partner and how they lived for several months, he most likely was satisfied with the answers he received.

Since Lawrence had introduced his curiosity about the subject, James took advantage of the original conversation they had earlier. When he was in a better place to explore the issue with Lawrence, he asked: "Do you remember a couple of months ago you asked me about how I lived with Bill and if we made love together the way Mommie and I used to?" Lawrence said, "Yes, why?" James replied, "Well, if there is ever anything you want to know about me or us, please ask me. You don't need to be afraid or embarrassed and you have a right to accurate information. You may hear things, especially at school that confuse you or worry you, so don't hesitate to call me or ask me when I come to visit." Sounding reassured, Lawrence replied, "Okay, I will."

Little more was shared on that occasion, but the groundwork had been laid for a secure relationship around this subject. Over the next two years Lawrence had a number of questions about incidences at school. These included a female classmate who revealed her Mom was lesbian, some kids teased her and Lawrence took up for her. Although it felt good to stick up for her, he was still hurt by being in that minority group. He had since seen and heard things on television that raised questions for him. During all of those experiences Lawrence has readily opened up to his father and asked about what he wanted to know.

We encourage trying to establish this type of relationship with your children. In most cases it makes the entire process easier over the long run. This process started for Lawrence when he was seven, yet he was able to share on a rather complex level. We realize every case has its unique circumstances and this can serve only as a general guideline for seven and eight-year-old children.

Not every case involving a gay parent coming out to his children is complicated. Although we are reporting most of these cases from our professional practices, not all situations require professional intervention. In fact, most cases with a little preplanning and preparation, evolve very successfully with little or no outside intervention.

**Case Study**

Such is the case of Mark, a six-year-old whose mother, June, came out to him when he was only four. June's partner, Marta, was a physical therapist who had cared for Mark after some corrective surgery for a congenital hip. During his convalescence and therapy, Mark became very fond of Marta. As it happened, Marta and June had a mutual attraction to one another and during this time had started to date. Marta had a rather large family of her own, but they were all grown and out of the home. As the relationship between Marta and June progressed, so did the relationship between Mark and Marta. Soon it was time to leave the hospital and Mark became very despondent over his separation from Marta.

While at home Mark made many comments about visiting with Marta again. He became so intense about wanting to see Marta again, he began feigning an illness hoping to go to the hospital again.

June was pleased that Mark liked Marta so much. However, she had never discussed her sexuality with him so she didn't know how she would explain Marta if anything further developed. Since the divorce Mark's

father had been very supportive. He knew June was lesbian, but felt that had no bearing on her having custody of Mark. During that time his life was very complicated with business matters, and he felt it best for Mark
to be with his mother.

June met with Marta and told her about Mark's
strong attachment to her. Since their relationship was
growing stronger every day, things seemed perfect for a
"move-in" type of relationship. June and Marta collectively decided it would be best if they were upfront with
Mark from the beginning. Taking into consideration
his age, four years, they rehearsed what they would tell
Mark.

Prior to coming out, June asked him, "What do you
think it means to be married?" Mark quickly answered, "Like you and Daddy used to be." Then June
asked, "Do you know what it means to be divorced?" To
that Mark replied, "Not really. All I know is that you and
Daddy have one, so you don't live together anymore."

Affirming his answers, June asked, "Do you know
what it means to be in love with someone?" His response, a little on the shy side was, "Getting mushy and
all that stuff." Wanting to introduce a more mature concept of love, June asked, "Is that how you think Daddy
and I used to be?" Thinking for a moment, Mark said,
"No that was different. You and Daddy were special to
each other. More like Gram and Gran (his grandparents)." [Note that Mark left out the word love in association with his parents and grandparents. Earlier he
had used the term "mushy" in reference to love. It is
usually during the late preschool years we begin to
tease youngsters about having their first girlfriend or
boyfriend. It is not unusual for children of this age to
not associate love between two adults as the foundation
for a relationship. Yet, they readily associate love between parent and child as being a special nurturing
bond.] Feeling that he understood that concept, June
asked, "Is there anyone that you like very much?" "Yes,"
Mark replied, "I like Larry (his best friend at day care) a
whole lot. Is that what you mean?" "Well, sort of." June
replied pensively, not knowing exactly how to carry this
analogy through. "You probably like Larry a lot and that

is good, but would you want to live with him all the time?" "No, I get tired of him sometimes and want to be with my other friends," Mark said. Hopefully back on the right track, June said, "Yeah. That is more what good friends are like. Sometimes you want to be around them and other times you want to be alone. Then there are some people you just want to be around all of the time." Excited, Mark exclaimed, "Like Marta. I would like to be around her all of the time." Then hoping not to confuse the issue, June told Mark, "I feel that way about Marta, too. I would like her around all of the time. I feel about her almost the same way I felt about Daddy. Do you understand that?" Sounding a bit confused Mark replied, "I'm not sure. Does that mean you love her like you used to love Daddy?" "Yes, I guess I do love her in a special way, kind of like Daddy, but I still love your Daddy, just in a different way," June concluded.

Feeling that Mark had a starting grasp on the concept, June phoned Marta and said she had broken the ice on the subject. She was not sure how much he understood, but he did not appear to be disturbed by what they had talked about. She felt that she had overloaded him with information and was almost making him try to understand concepts that she was not sure she could explain even if he were older. June wanted to give that introduction a few weeks to sink in before introducing the possibility of Marta coming to live with them. During that time Mark asked several questions about relationships, what happens when two people stop living together, etc., but he never brought up the same sex aspect, or special feelings, or the affection between June and Marta.

Feeling some trepidation about Mark's lack of questions or feedback after their initial conversation, June called Marta and said she thought it was time to test the waters again. Feeling the need for some moral support, she asked Marta if she would come over for the next round of talks. Marta affirmed the request and the following, rather amazing thing happened. Just as soon as Marta came in the house, Mark burst out, "When are you going to move in and be my other Mother?!" Feeling somewhat dumbfounded, June and

Marta stared at each other not knowing what to say. Mark continued, "Mom said she liked you almost like Dad, so that means you are going to move in, right?"

Continuing to be amazed at Mark's words, Marta said, "We have talked about it but nothing is final."

Really not knowing where to go with the conversation, June said, "Mark, do you remember when we talked about Marta several weeks ago?" Mark gave a positive head nod. "Well, do you have any questions about that?" Mark replied, "No. You just said y'all had special feelings for each other, so I guess you like each other enough to always live together. So when do you move in, Marta?"

Feeling that Mark understood enough of what was going on, June concluded their conversation by saying, "Mark, if you ever want to ask me or Marta or Daddy or Gram and Gran any questions about feelings, please come to any of us. OK?" Mark nodded another affirmative response, and went on to show Marta around the house.

The coming out process continued almost as smoothly over the next two years. They did have to handle one awkward moment when Mark thought Marta would be occupying the spare bedroom. He also went through a minor crisis when he went to the first grade and again had to handle being in a single parent home. Once when drawing his family for art period, he drew figures representing himself labeled "me" and both Marta and June labeled as "Mother." When the teacher sent the drawing home wondering if Mark was confusing his "aunt" Marta with his mother, once again some explanations were in order.

June began the process much in the same way she originally did. She asked Mark, "Do you know Jerry's parents?" (Jerry was one of Mark's friends who was also from a divorced family and now had a step-mother). Mark confirmed that he knew Jerry's parents. June then asked, "Is Alice Jerry's real Mom?" Mark responded, "No, his real Mom lives in Denver." "She is his step-mom like in Cinderella, but she is not mean?" Mark replied, "She is someone who came to live with his Dad after the divorce."

By this time Mark's father had remarried. Mark inserted, "If I lived with Dad, Alice would be my step-mom, but since I don't Marta is my step-mom. Right?" "Well, it is sort of like that, but not everyone is going to understand that because a step-mom is usually someone who comes to live with your Dad, but not your Mom. If I got married to a man again, he would come to live with us and be your step-dad." Sounding slightly puzzled, Mark inquired, "so why isn't she my step-mom?" Not being able to come up with a better explanation, June concluded, "That sounds good enough for now. We'll talk more about this later."

This is an excellent example of using the language and analogies your child is familiar with. In this case, when Mark was both four and seven, he was not loaded down with extraneous information. Too much information will just slide off—but if your child keeps asking questions, keep supplying the answers as you are able. When children seem satisfied with a certain level of explanation, we encourage parents to leave it there, while leaving the door open for further information. You recall June's comment to Mark: "If you have any questions, feel free to ask" and "we'll talk more about this later."

All of the complexities of a relationship are hard to explain. Sometimes there are no real clear cut analogies to carry from a heretofore straight relationship to a gay relationship, especially when talking with very young children under the age of eight.

This is also a good example of how to introduce the subject. June asked Mark what he already knew about various relationship concepts, i.e., marriage and divorce, love and special feelings. By so doing, she could assess what Mark already knew and got the feel for his level of understanding. Frequently children of Mark's age fill in the missing parts on their own, and complete a concept without really understanding it all. Such was the case when he concluded Marta would be his step-mother. It may be several years before he can make more refined distinctions about relationships. But in June's words of wisdom, "That sounds good enough for now. We'll talk more about it later."

We should point out this example is not common for a four-year-old. Mark was an intelligent and precocious child. Because of his congenital hip problems he read a lot and spent an unusual amount of time in the presence of adults. Also, he was close to five when hospitalized and was there through his fifth birthday. He did not start to school until he was seven, so some of his responses were not typical of first graders. However, we have noticed that children who adjust readily to change demonstrate an advanced stage of maturity.

**Case Study**    Sometimes situations occur that cause several different issues to be managed at the same time. Two men, Mike and Gary, had been involved in a relationship for three years. Gary had two girls and one boy from a former relationship. His ex-wife, Mary, had custody, and he had every other weekend visitation.

During the divorce the gay issue was a minor point. There was some disagreement and discussion about visitation as it related to the gay issue, but most of the time there was no resolution to the concerns on either side; therefore, the issue went undiscussed most of the time. When Gary started to date Mike, Mary made threats about having the custody agreement revised and not let the children come to visit. Mike also was having a real problem with visitation. He felt the children intruded in his life and privacy, especially when they spent the weekend.

Gary had always been close to his children and wanted his relationship to remain as intact as possible. The conflict between Gary and Mike brought them into counseling. Except for trying to create a reason for Mike's existence in Gary's home, little was discussed with the children about the living arrangement. The three children, David, nine, Sue, six, and Joan, five, enjoyed visiting their father and Mike. Most of the weekends were like holidays for them with trips to the show, amusement park and museum. Mike felt Gary was overcompensating with the children to cover their relationship. He felt the kids were being kept so busy with activities to look forward to during their visits, that they never had time to make sense out of the relationship.

During some of the early sessions we discussed what role Mike wanted to have in the children's lives. He was content to have none, but felt if he took that role, he would be more and more excluded from Gary. Although their bedroom was off limits to the children, Mike felt crowded when the children were there. He also did not like all of the pretending that went on between he and Gary in the children's presence.

We discussed the ramifications of coming out to the children. Gary felt Mary would blow up if that happened. During one of their arguments over the gay issue and the children, Mary threatened, "If the kids ever find out you are gay, I'll get an order denying visitation so fast it will make your head spin. I know it is important for them to have a continued relationship with you as their father, but I swear, if you expose them to that filth and perversion, that is the last you'll ever see of them. Furthermore, if the kids find out, then you can damn well bet your parents, grandparents, friends and employer will all know everything about you!!"

Gary, for a number of reasons had not chosen to come out to any more than a small number of gay friends. He felt very vulnerable to his ex-wife's threats. He found himself in the proverbial catch-22. We discussed trying to negotiate the point with his wife. Since she was in the health care profession, we suggested she discuss the issues with some of her colleagues who were experienced in this area. Mary did agree to talk to some of them, but firmly stated nothing could change her mind.

Unfortunately, that opportunity never came to pass. During one of their weekends, the children were alone in the house while Gary and Mike were on the patio fixing hamburgers. Mike was finishing up with the pool's spring cleaning and had asked the kids to stay inside since he was using some caustic chemicals in the cleaning solution. The kids kept wanting to come outside and play, but fearing an accident Gary said for them to watch television for a while. Still trying to persuade Gary to let them come out they complained there was nothing on television except ball games. Gary had purchased some videotapes for the kids and told them to put one of those on the VCR. While the kids were choosing between *Superman* and *Star Wars*, David came out and said something was being recorded on the tape in the den. In an effort to cut short the negotiations to come outside, Gary made an exception to using the television in their bedroom. The children, feeling a victory at hand in getting to use the television in the "forbidden" room, ran into the house. Gary called after them, "Don't mess up anything. Supper will be ready in about 20 minutes, then you all can go swimming."

About half an hour passed and the children did not emerge from the house. Gary called them a couple of times, but they did not respond. After 45 minutes went by, Gary stuck his head in the back door and said, "No supper, no swimming. I don't want to have to call you kids again." With that last, firm-sounding warning, the children emerged. There was something strange about their demeanor. They were overly quiet. This was extremely unusual in the face of the opportunity to go swimming. Shortly after supper, David complained, "My stomach hurts. I think we should go home." Sensing something wrong, Gary felt his forehead and said, "You don't have any fever. What is the matter?" The two girls were very quiet. Gary asked them, "Is there something wrong with you two?" Sue responded, "I don't feel good either. I want to go back to Mother's."

Assuming they had a fight among themselves and were now out of sorts, Gary agreed to take them home. Mike thought that was a good idea. He offered to stay behind and clean up. Actually he was rather relieved they were leaving. He was angry over Gary's offer to use the television in their bedroom. He felt his last sanctuary of privacy was now in the kid's domain. Stewing in his anger he continued to clean up the supper dishes. In an effort to defuse his feelings he called a couple of friends and spent the next hour on the phone.

Meanwhile, Gary took the kids home to a neighboring suburban town a few miles away. During the drive he tried to pry out of the kids what their fight was about. He never liked the kids to return to their Mother's upset or in a bad mood fearing Mary would think "one of those gay things" had happened. In spite of Gary's best efforts, the kids continued to tell him nothing was wrong, they just did not feel well. When he dropped the kids off he and Mary spoke briefly. Seeing the subdued demeanor of the kids Mary said, "What did you do to them this time?" Gary responded sharply, "Nothing, they just had too much of a good time for a change. They are just tired, that's all!"

With those closing remarks, Gary stormed out of the house. There was nothing unusual about this homecoming or departure. Regardless how the kids came home, there was always some complaint waiting. He was accused of spoiling them, making them irresponsible, feeding them the wrong foods, etc. He realized none of this was true and this was just the way he and Mary would grind their respective axes with one another. On the way home, he stopped to do some necessary shopping.

A few minutes later back at their house, Mike was still on the phone. He was just getting ready to hang up when the operator cut in on the line and requested release for an emergency call from Mary. Fearing something had happened to Gary and the kids, Mike released the line immediately and spoke to Mary. Her voice was unusually strained when she said, "Let me speak to Gary right now!" Mike responded somewhat concerned, "Isn't he over there?" "Hell no!" Mary screamed. In a more confused and concerned tone, Mike asked, "When did he leave?" Still in a near hysterical tone Mary said, "He has had plenty of time to get there, I don't know what in the hell is going on, but when he gets there, you tell him to get on this phone to me NOW!"

The relationship between Mike and Mary had never been good. They were usually cordial to one another, but the tension between them was always evident. Mike still sensing some grave concern for Mary asked, "What in the world is wrong? Has something happened to the kids?" Mary screamed back, "You'd better believe it!" and slammed down the phone.

Being rather concerned and equally puzzled, Mike hung up the phone. He finished up in the kitchen, then made a couple of calls to friends who Gary might have stopped off to visit. Upon discovering that no one had heard from him he assumed he would be home shortly. Mike then proceeded to the bedroom to see what needed to be done after the kids had been unleashed on it. When he walked in to the room and saw the *Superman* and *Star Wars* videotapes on the bed, a chilling thought flashed through his mind. He and Gary had purchased a couple of explicit gay erotic videotapes. He vaguely thought one of them had been left in the VCR in their bedroom. Everything for a moment seemed to move in slow motion. At first he was relieved to see the television off. That relief was soon destroyed when he noticed the "on" indicator illuminated on the VCR. Dreading his next task, he turned on the television and to his dismay, there was the explicit movie. He had mixed emotions of rage at Gary for letting the kids use the bedroom, fear at what would happen between the kids, Gary and Mary, some scary relief that it might be over between Gary and the kids, and an overwhelming fear that this crisis would break them up. He was hoping that perhaps the kids had not seen the movie. Perhaps they had pushed the on button and became distracted with other things to get into, but who was he fooling? The kids acted so strange at supper, then Mary's hysterical call. He was sure the inevitable had happened.

It seemed like an eternity before Gary drove up. Mike felt more unprepared for this than anything he could remember. He didn't know whether to jump Gary's case or to be supportive. He got a chance to be neither, for just as Gary walked in the door, the phone rang.

Putting the grocery bag down and throwing a kiss in Mike's direction, Gary answered the phone with his familiar gesturing voice, "Helllooo, Gar here. How may we be of service?" "Listen, you bastard, you'd better contact your lawyer!" said an anonymous voice that Gary immediately recognized as Mary's. Then there was silence on the other end of the line.

"Well!" Gary said, "I wonder what that was all about?"

Threats about seeing your lawyer were also not new in the ongoing feud between Gary and Mary. Looking at Mike's ashen face, Gary said, "And what is the matter with you? First the kids, then Mary and now you. What's up?"

Mike, in a somber voice replied, "You'd better come here. Who was that on the phone." "Mary, I think. She said for the hundredth time for me to get with my lawyer. Wonder what burr is under her tail now?" Gary responded. Still in a somber voice, Mike replied, "That might be good advice. Come here and take a look."

Mike went to the VCR and pushed the eject button. Gary was looking at the *Star Wars* and *Superman* tapes on the bed and began to have the same thoughts Mike had experienced a few moments earlier. "Don't tell me . . ." Gary said with a vacant stare into space. "Well, the cat is out of the bag." Mike responded with an equally bland stare.

Both sat in silence for a few minutes, then Gary said, "What do you think she'll do?"

A lot happened after that eventful day. There were several problems facing the children, the least of which was the isolated exposure to explicit material. However, because of the material, they had been exposed to frank sexuality, explicit erotica, same sex relationships, their father's sexuality, and their mother's rage over the event.

Our intervention in the case was small from that point on. Mary did file the suit she threatened to earlier. She petitioned the court to revoke all contact and visitation with Gary. She asked for triple child support to pay for therapy for the children. During one of the first few volleys fired at one another, smoke screens were put up around the coming out and sexuality issues. Mary accused Gary of being a careless parent, and that combined with his perversions should be reason enough to never see the children again. Gary accused Mary of being a negligent parent in that she did not teach the children about privacy and had prevented him from talking about human sexuality and its variations with the children.

When the charges and counter charges slowed down

a bit, we encouraged both parents to look at the real issues. The children indeed had been exposed to explicit material, and this was the result of poor judgment and planning on both their parts. The children were unfairly being sheltered from real events in their lives. Their father was indeed gay and living with another man, both of whom had a heretofore fairly stable relationship with the children. For the past few years everyone was trying to pretend that these things did not exist; therefore, there would be nothing to handle with the children. Now that the kids had seen some of the material that raised questions for them, both parents were trying to pretend this did not happen.

As long as they could play that game, they did not have to handle the current issue. Our position was that they no longer were afforded the luxury of avoidance. These children had some real issues before them, and had a right to some responsible answers.

Little action was taken on our position until the matter came to trial. After we presented evidence that the children had not been unduly harmed by the material, we were able to defuse some of the erroneous focus on the videotape and concentrate on the issues surrounding the children. We encouraged both parents to make a concerted effort to attend to the questions the children did indeed have. We explained that many children are unwittingly exposed to explicit erotica. This occasionally happens by picking up a discarded explicit magazine, viewing adult material that the parents may have, inadvertently turn on a cable channel that has explicit adult viewing, etc. There is no more "damage" done by one type of material versus another, unless it contained violent, sadistic scenes (none of which were contained in the tape viewed). Since these were real life events that children are exposed to, we encouraged the parents to get with the therapist that had been chosen for the children, and resolve any questions or confusion the children might have.

In the final analysis the judge hearing the visitation issue agreed with us. He emphatically did state that the incident probably could have been prevented, and that it also represented poor preplanning. He further stated he felt the parents were letting their respective battles get in the way of the best interests of the children, and ordered both parents to therapy. After reviewing the report of the children's therapist, he felt no other professional intervention was necessary for the children, except perhaps to defuse the parents' conflicts as they affected the children. And finally, the judge felt that the request for restricted visitation was not supported by the evidence, but firmly warned Gary that a similar episode brought to his attention would be dealt with in a grave manner.

Our rationale in presenting this case is to point out how avoiding real issues in your life might result in a complex maze like this one. This is not an isolated case. While not every case deals with explicit erotic material, in fact they are in the extreme minority, we do have other telltale material and experiences to draw from. On several occasions issues have developed around a child's discovering a non-sexual publication, like *Growing Up Gay* or *Society and the Homosexual,* or belonging to a gay political group and being on their mailing lists, etc.

We feel children should be prepared for many of these life events, by having such a relationship with their parents, gay or straight, where they can go openly with their questions. Once these issues are handled in a healthy and constructive fashion, they usually cease to be major issues. Soon they become common events in your children's lives, and cease to be issues.

**Case Study**

There are many family constellations where children of vastly different ages are involved in the coming out process. Several years ago, we worked with a lesbian couple who had been together for 15 years. They had eight children between them. When they first got together the eldest child was ten and the youngest less than one year. Jane, the older of the two, had three girls and two boys. Marge, the younger member of the couple, had two boys and one girl. For most of the relationship, the subject of homosexuality had not been brought up. Except for the oldest child, Jackie, who was ten at the time they got together, most of the children were busy dealing with the divorce, the structure of a completely new and much larger family, and two female heads of the household. Over the years, there had been a lot of issues raised over how best to parent all these children. Some of the parenting chores were assigned to the older children since both parents worked. Due to all these ever changing challenges to the family, the unit as such never got around to facing the lesbian issue. During all these years, the two women shared the same bedroom, did virtually everything together and shared the parenting duties equally over the family, not to just their own children. Both women decided on the same last name; therefore, the parenting lines at school were even muddled.

The older children fairly well assimilated what was going on, but still nothing was ever said. A rather indirect and unexpected event caused the subject to get discussed.

Jane and Marge were acquaintances with another lesbian couple, who also had children living with them. The fact of lesbianism had filtered back to one of the ex-husbands, who filed suit to get custody of his daughter. This event made the news and when Jane and Marge heard about it, there was some discussion among themselves about the particulars of the case, but nothing of merit was said to the family as a whole. One night during a news update on the suit, Judy, now 12, asked if their fathers were going to take them back in the same way. When Judy asked this, all of the family was in front of the television set, and a strange silence fell over everyone.

Jane and Marge had discussed the potential of such an event in their relationship. However, both fathers had expressed no interest in having custody at the time of the divorce, and over the years had minimal contact with the family. In recent years there had been no contact from the fathers. Both Jane and Marge knew there was no chance for trouble from their ex-husbands, so gave a simple no to the question, "Are our Daddies going to take us away too (referring to the news item)?"

Jane and Marge just looked at each other for a moment knowing there was more information and understanding behind the question than was asked on the surface. There was that awkward silence that meant—there is a lot to handle there and do we want to handle it? Also there was the consideration of all the children being present to think about. When this particular event took place, Judy, the youngest, was only 12. The oldest child was then in her early twenties. The decision at the time was to put up a smoke screen and Marge replied, "Oh, your fathers don't even know where you are. When was the last time you heard from them? They did not even send you Christmas gifts, and heaven knows how long it has been since they sent any child support. Sandy (the oldest) has been working since she was 16 to help out financially. Boy, some fathers they turned out to be. Let me see if I can find the last letter Jack (Marge's ex-husband) wrote to us. It's been so long, I don't really remember where I put it, if I kept it at all." On leaving the room Marge motioned to Jane saying, "Come on, help me look for those letters."

When in the privacy of their own room, Marge and Jane just stared at each other, not knowing where to start. Their lives had become so routine, they had forgotten that their family was different and that the difference had never been discussed with their children. Over the next three years when the family unit came into therapy, a variety of partial coming out experiences happened to the family.

Jane decided she needed to tell her children right off. They were old enough to leave the family anyway, and probably had a better handle on what the other children knew, if anything.

Sandy had indeed figured out their relationship a number of years ago. There appeared to be an unspoken code among the children to not discuss their moms' relationship, so for the most part it was never mentioned. Occasionally Sandy would be asked by other younger children if she thought Jane and Marge would ever get married again. When the questions were first raised, Sandy thought it was out of the curiosity about another father. Later the concern seemed to be that a remarriage by either Jane or Marge would break up the family. Therefore, something that might have been wished for earlier, was later viewed as a potential threat to the integrity of the family. Sandy also had taken on a protective role for the younger children. She believed all such lesbian relationships didn't last; therefore, she would have to stick around and take care of the kids during the breakup(s).

Marge's two boys had some difficult adjusting to do. While the previously mentioned child custody was getting a lot of press, some of the children at the school started to tease Marge's boys, Joe and Tom. By now everyone at their school knew Joe and Tom had two mothers. Both of them had come to their school as the primary parent. The children started to tease them about having "lesbos" for parents. Both of the boys were rather stout in stature, so many fights erupted over the teasing they received. Since Joe and Tom were embarrassed over what the children at school were saying, they usually told the teachers and principal that there was no reason for the fights. When Jane and Marge would question them about the fights, they would equally clam up and say there was nothing going on. The fights were just games that got rough, then out of hand.

Because of the lack of intervention, the boys continued to get in trouble at school and started to act out in other ways. Although the boys were only average students, they always passed. Now they were bringing home failing marks. Since these were the first failing grades for either of them, Jane and Marge felt the situation would improve. Unfortunately, the grade situation only deteriorated. Several parent conferences were called at school. Although both women showed up at the conferences together, nothing was ever mentioned about the family unit or their relationship. It was not until the family came into therapy that the boys revealed they were having problems.

During the course of working with the family, neither of the boys had any particular bad feelings about the lesbian relationship between their mothers. They felt unsupported when the trouble began, but assigned no blame for the lack of support. They felt that they could not bring up the subject or the real reasons they were being teased. Since no one ever mentioned anything about Jane and Marge's relationship, they assumed the subject was off limits. At times Joe and Tom got close to talking about it among themselves, but never got very detailed. Since they never had experienced any other type of family in their conscious memory, they could not imagine things being different than they were. They were relieved at being able to share the information in the family and felt more supported now. However, that did not soften the problem at school. When their mothers were called "lesbos," they felt their parents were being attacked. This became a very personal thing for them, especially Tom, who was very close to both Jane and Marge. He continued to get into fights and do poorly at school.

Judy, the one who more or less innocently opened the can of worms, took her inquiries to school. She and her classmates frequently and at length talked about the custody case. Not fully understanding the analogy between her situation and the family on the news, she did not realize the depth to which she was absorbing the ideas shared among her friends. With all the authority that every 12-year-old can muster, her friends assured them that all the children in "any home like that" would be taken out. She was cited fantasy examples about how the policeman comes to your door and takes the kids away, even if they don't want to go. After sharing some of this information, Judy began to see the parallel between the case on the news and her own living situation. She became fearful that she would be dragged out against her will and sent to some foster home, so she began to stay at her grandmother's house a lot. At first this did not seem out of the ordinary, because Judy stayed over there frequently. Her grandmother lived around the corner from them, and she and her grandmother were very close.

Before long both Marge and Jane could tell something was wrong with Judy. She never usually stayed more than one night at a time, except on weekends.

Now she began to extend weekend stays into Monday and Tuesday. Secretly she had begun to move some of her belongings to Grandmother's. When asked why she wanted to stay at Grandmother's, she would reply, "We're working on something together." At other times the story would grow to, "Grandmother isn't feeling well, and she asked me to help her out for a few days." Of course, when Jane and Marge inquired about Grandmother's health, they would discover that it was Judy who had asked to stay over for the extended time. Since she was back and forth between houses several times a day, nothing had ever been said until the inconsistency of the stories was discovered.

After being told she would have to spend less time with Grandmother, Judy moved back home, but continued to keep some of her things there just in case she had to move in quickly. It later came out that Judy thought if she was at her grandmother's house when the policeman came, they could not take her away. She was very relieved to learn that the advice her friend had given her was far from accurate.

During the course of working with this family, all of the age groups had to be taken into consideration. We also were amazed about how an unspoken code developed, where the rule was to not talk about Jane and Marge's relationship. Each child more or less formed their own opinion of what was the structure of the relationship, but did nothing to validate or invalidate what they understood. Since this family was thrown together with the ready-made age differences, it was impossible to set the entire group down and come out in one setting. Remember, the youngest was about one year old when the couple got together. When the family came into therapy the age spread was from almost 11 to the mid-twenties. Also it was such a large family, it was easy to get caught up in day to day matters. A lot of time passed quickly and the problems developed as a natural process of just being exposed to our society and news items.

Our suggestion for anyone with a family unit with diverse age groups is to at first take each child aside and explain things at their level of understanding as preparation for a more general family conferences that include everyone. This is certainly a case where a diversity of situations will exist and a lot of flexibility will help. Also as the older children have some good, factual information, they will be of help to the younger members.

As the family of Marge and Jane worked through the coming out process, Sandy left home and was married. The two remaining older children left home for college. Tom and Joe improved in school, but Tom continued to have acting-out problems. We are not sure if this was a problem secondary to the family stress or because he was entering the rebellion phase that effects many teens. Tom later was put into a private school and improved considerably. Judy continued to spend a lot of time at her grandmother's but overcame the fear that she would be taken out of the home by a policeman. When she was 16, she asked if she could move in with her grandmother permanently. She said it was because the home was too crowded and noisy and that she had her own room. Permission was granted for the move. Judy continued to live back and forth, though she declared her permanent residence as her grandmother's house. The remaining children were never very active in therapy and their behavior remained constant throughout therapy and after the family stopped therapy.

For various reasons some individuals feel that coming out to their children will destroy the family. Therefore, they prefer not to come out until the children are grown, out of high school, or somewhat more on their own. This particular choice has varying outcomes. Needless to say, the gay parent of a heterosexual union must live a facade for many years, and if he or she is sexually active, that means there usually are affairs outside the marriage. It becomes increasingly imperative for the parent to keep this side of his or her life secret. This becomes increasingly difficult, since obvious strains start to develop within the marital relationship.

**Case Study**     We have worked with several cases of this type. Our most recent one involved a gay man who had remained married for over 25 years. During the last seven years, the marriage, as a marriage, had all but ended. The couple had two daughters, now in their late teens. The father had moved out of the house, but neither parent had filed for divorce. The father was now living with a male "roommate" for "financial reasons"; however, this "roommate" had been his lover for several years.

The relationship between the father and his lover had broken up over the stresses of the dangling marriage. This breakup greatly added to the father's burden, and his stress became so great he became very depressed and sought therapy.

We will call this individual Joe. He came to our office extremely depressed and had frequent suicidal thoughts. Joe was convinced everything was over for him. He had a lot of guilt about the years of unfaithfulness to his wife. He was miserable about the recent breakup with his lover, Phil. His greatest pain was his distant relationship with his two daughters, especially the oldest, to whom he felt the closest.

Joe wanted more than anything for his oldest daughter, Faith, to understand his behavior and lifestyle. They had always been close, even after he had moved out of the house. Over the years they had shared almost every secret a father and daughter can. Even with that history, though, Joe felt his daughter would never accept his homosexuality, especially in light of the way he had treated the family over the past seven years.

After some discussion about the worst that could happen—which was that his daughter could only totally reject him—Joe decided to tell her. After all, even if she did reject him, their relationship would not be a lot different from its current status.

Joe, being very nervous about telling Faith about being gay, decided to invite her out for a holiday weekend. He was trying to set a high-spirited atmosphere for coming out. Faith, sensing the tension of the moment and trying to help break the ice, announced, "If it will help, I know why you and Mom split." Since this was out of the blue, Joe thought about trying to deflect the sudden disclosing direction they were headed toward. Having made an agreement in therapy to tell the truth, however, and take advantage of any opening by Faith, he replied, "What do you think is wrong between your mother and me?" To that Faith replied, "I don't think anything is wrong between you and Mom, you can still be great friends. It is your hiding that is the problem. We all know what has been going on between you and Phil. Long before you became "roommates" we figured out that you and he were lovers, and even if you weren't, you should have been."

Joe was overwhelmed with the amount of accurate information that Faith was sharing with him, especially since he assumed all along, very little, if anything was known about his sexuality. Faith indicated her realization when he and Phil went through a short-term breakup by sharing, "You moped around the house like a spanked puppy. You would spend hours on the phone with him having your half-baked conversations, hoping that none of us would guess what was happening. You sounded like me when I broke up with Mack. Since you and Mother never liked him, I was afraid to tell you that we had been dating. You both figured that out pretty quick, if I remember correctly."

In a situation like this we encourage parents to take advantage of the situation and without breaking confidences between people, use a discussion like this one to find out how other family members are handling the situation. Joe asked, "How is your mother handling all this?" Faith replied, "She has been handling it fine for a long time now. At first she was angry because you lied about everything, and then she was afraid to ask you about anything, although I don't know why. We don't talk about it all the time, but have talked about it more since you moved out. Sue (the younger daughter) has not taken it so well, but you know her, she never takes anything that is different well. Sometimes she says she hates you, other times she says you are sick, but I guess you notice she never forgets your birthday or Father's Day or anything. I guess she'll get over it when she gets older. She usually doesn't like for us to talk about it."

We encouraged Joe to continue with the coming out

process with Sue. She appeared to be more accepting than she displayed to Faith and her mother. Her sending cards and gifts on special occasions indicated that she wanted to keep the relationship alive. Joe reported that he wanted to come out to her and admitted her acceptance was not as important as Faith's, but he still was fearful of an emotionally charged rejection.

Joe chose to go home to tell Sue so she would have access to her mother if she was unduly upset by his coming out. Sue was much less open than Faith and considerably more reserved in her support of Joe's lifestyle. While coming out Joe said, "The last thing I want is to cause you more pain than you have gone through already, so if you don't want to talk about this, just tell me and I'll go." Sue replied, "It's not that I don't want to talk about it. It is just that I don't know what there is to say. It seems that all everyone wants to do is to talk about it. Faith and Mom even have laughed at queers on television, dressed up like women and trying to be women. I think that is wrong!"

Since it was obvious that Sue either had some misinformation or a stereotypic notion about gay men, Joe asked, "Do you think all gay men, 'queers,' as you put it, dress up and act like women?" Sue replied a little on the defensive, "No, not all of them, but most of them do. They do other things like S & M and stuff. I get so embarrassed when I think about my friends' reaction if they knew about you."

In an effort to impart some accurate information to Sue and still remain on a personal level, he said, "You have seen Phil around here lots of times, and used to enjoy going out with us. He and I are still the same people. I realize Phil and I are having some problems, but we are trying to solve those." An issue appeared to be beginning to develop for Sue, and she said, "That is just the thing. You want to work things out with Phil and not with Mom. I think you are being unfair. You and she should try to work things out and stay together. I get sick when I think that you feel the same way about Phil as you did about Mother. If you knew that you were 'that way,' why did you ever get married?"

Joe was now at the root of Sue's discomfort. She was

the innocent victim of a lot of misinformation and stereotypic notions of what gays are like. A long and difficult journey had begun for them both. They continued to have periodic times when they would get together and share feelings. Sue continued to send cards and gifts to Joe on special occasions.

There is still some tension between Joe and Sue. Each visit gets easier, but it is obvious there are issues between them that need resolving and that will take time. Sue reports that while she wished things were different for her father, she is glad that she has had the truth verified. At first she was very angry that her father came out to her because she felt it encouraged his homosexuality and contributed to the final breakup. After some time, she started to enjoy her relationship with her father more since the unspoken barrier was out of the way. She is now also willing to examine the misinformation she had about gays and their lifestyle.

In coming out to children over the age of ten, there are some unexpected issues that can arise. In the case just cited, both daughters were old enough to have heard a lot of information some accurate and some not, about gays. The younger daughter had developed a belief system about the accuracy of her information and was very upset when she tried to put her father into unacceptable roles. Both girls were going through a very self-conscious stage in their own development and were overly sensitive to the opinions of their peers. Faith, being almost 20 during most of the early coming out stage between her and Joe, was leaving that sensitive phase; therefore, the transition was easier for her. Faith also had other things going for her that made the transition easier. She was attractive, popular at school, and had a strong relationship with her boyfriend, who was also encouraging acceptance of Joe. Sue, on the other hand, was somewhat withdrawn. The few friends she did have were fairly conservative in their ideas and opinions, and Sue was afraid of losing them if they found out about her father.

In trying to help Joe with these family differences, we encouraged him to take the position that these things were phases in Sue's life. While we did not want to diminsh the importance of these phases in her life, we did want him to give serious consideration to the foundation being laid for the relationship that would span the rest of their lives. This concept helped Joe press forward in the coming out process.

Sue says she is glad that she knows, but still wishes it was different. She hopes that time will help her understand and accept him better. She does accept her father as he is. While she feels that he is wrong, she does not feel that he is bad. We reminded Joe of the phrase in the book, "acceptance is different than approval."

If custody is granted a gay parent, it is usually the lesbian instead of the gay man who gets custody of the children. This usually happens only when the judge does not know the mother is lesbian. Therefore, we have worked with a large number of lesbian women who have primary custody of their children. Because of a variety of circumstances, many women choose not to tell their children. Frequently, it is out of fear that they will lose their children if their ex-husband finds out. Sometimes there is concern that a parent, grandparent or an in-law will attempt some legal action to terminate her custody. We understand these circumstances and have addressed them elsewhere in the book. Nevertheless, many women are in a good position to tell their children, but they are dealing with their own pain and tend to avoid sharing this information.

**Case Study**    We have a case in point here involving a long-term relationship between two women. Susan, who was married previously, has an 11-year-old daughter, Kay. Her partner, Jeri, has never been married and this is her first relationship with anyone. Susan divorced her husband when Kay was two, and the next year met Jeri. Shortly thereafter, Jeri moved in and came into therapy because Kay had begun to act out at school. Since Kay had been a bright student, Susan and Jeri began to worry about Kay's failing grades. Prior to this time Jeri and Kay had a warm and close relationship, much like that of a second mother. Recently Kay had begun to defy her openly, frequently daring punishment and screaming that Jeri could not touch her because she was not her mother. Moreover, the situation between Kay and her mother was not much better.

After the initial interviews, we discovered the primary feud was between Kay and her mother. Kay was insisting on a lock for her door like her mother and Jeri had. After a few minutes of discussing privacy issues, knocking on a closed door before entering, etc., we asked Kay why she thought the lock was on her mother's door. Bypassing the privacy issue, Kay said, "So I won't know they are 'queer!'" then she began to cry. "Would having a lock on your door help?" we inquired. Between sobs, Kay said, "No, it's just that I used to get to go in and sit on their bed and watch television and everything. Jeri thinks she is so smart because she gets to go in there and have the door locked." "Is that why you have been fighting with Jeri?" we inquired. Sounding a bit defensive Kay responded, "No, it is more than that. You see, they are always fighting. I sometimes come home in the afternoon after school, and I can hear them fighting and hear things being said about me, but as soon as I walk in the door, they act like nothing is going on. I am afraid Jeri doesn't like me anymore and wants me to live with Daddy, but I don't want to leave. I don't want to go live with Daddy. If I don't go to live with Daddy, I think she is going to tell my Mom that she will leave."

Fortunately, nothing could have been farther from the truth. While Jeri did not enjoy the fights, she certainly did not want to leave the relationship or Kay. Jeri did not understand the sudden change in Kay's attitude and behavior. She felt that she had always gotten along very well with Kay and they had been a family for so long, she felt more like a mother to Kay than a stepparent or friend. Much of her role over the years had taken on the characteristics of a parent.

Susan and Jeri admitted they had strong differences of opinion regarding the coming out issue as it involved Kay. Jeri's position was that Kay had long since figured it out and was handling it in her own way. Susan was adamant that they had been so careful not to express anything towards one another that Kay could interpret as being gay; therefore, she could not possibly know. That was the primary reason for the lock on the door. Susan had become worried that Kay was at a curious age and might start to look around their room and discover something that might reveal their sexuality.

During the latter interview we asked Kay what she meant when she used the term "queer." She responded "I mean gay or 'homos.'" We further inquired, "Do you know what that is?" Looking a little puzzled, Kay said, "I don't know really what they do, but it is like two guys living together in Capital Hill (a predominantly gay neighborhood in their hometown). We never talk about it and they think I don't know. All of their friends are like that. I figured out something was going on since I was in the first grade, but I didn't know what you called it then. I don't really care about that, I still love them both, but I don't want to live with my Dad." Then she began to cry silently again.

In spite of our best efforts to convince Susan of Kay's rather sophisticated knowledge of her mother's lifestyle and her acceptance of it as okay, she still was not convinced of the safety of openly sharing the facts with Kay. Even after sharing Kay's fears that their fights were about sending her to her father's and that Jeri no longer liked her, Susan was unmoved about clearing up the mystery for Kay. Even though she anticipated that the situation would continue on a downhill course and get much worse, Susan chose to take the family out of therapy. Jeri continued to come in for several more appointments in an effort to figure out some way to ease the tension. Our advice to her was to try to convince Susan of the importance of clearing up the mistaken communication and notions that Kay had, especially in light of Kay's notion that she and Jeri had any sort of unresolvable problem between them. During these later interviews Jeri revealed Susan had always had a major problem fearing people might find out she was lesbian. She took great pains to make sure her straight and gay friends never met. She was also antagonistic about "gay and coming out" movements and political efforts. We urged Jeri to encourage Susan to get involved in some women's support groups that helped women explore their feelings about themselves.

Susan, however, refused Jeri's efforts to help. We advised Jeri that her hands were tied if Susan was refusing to let her try to intervene with Kay, since Jeri had no legal ties to Kay. Shortly thereafter, Jeri dropped out of therapy. Several months after her termination from therapy, Jeri called to inform us that she and Susan had broken up. She felt that in everyone's best interest she should clear the air between herself and Kay. She told Kay she still loved her very much and was sorry that they had argued with one another over the past several months. She hoped they could always be friends. She went on to explain as best as she could about being a lesbian. When Kay asked if her mother also was lesbian, Jeri responded, "She'll have to tell you that herself."

Jeri left the relationship, and after that account, we lost track of Susan and Kay. We do not know if the issue between them was resolved or not.

Our effort here is to encourage parents to take advantage of opportunities like this. Sometimes the first person a child will tell that she knows about her parents being gay is a close friend, aunt, uncle or therapist. This provides an excellent opportunity to pick up with the information your child already has. This information is just awaiting confirmation from that parent.

Unfortunately, the case just discussed involved a woman who was uncomfortable with her sexuality. She resisted any effort to make her comfort level better. In this case, and in so many other similar cases, the child was bearing a great portion of the parent's problem.

We again remind you of our position, that it is the parent's duty to bring up these issues with your children. If, as in this and some of our other examples, your child has already figured things out at his level, this is a great opportunity to use the child's inquiring comments to start the coming out process.

Since it is our desire to make coming out as healthy and an exemplary a process as possible, we encourage answering your children's questions as honestly as possible. Refrain from ducking the issue or sending up smoke screens. Discuss things at their level of comprehension and do not try to do this all in one setting.

# Your Adult Children—
# Another Story

As strange as it may seem, many parents of adult children have an even more difficult time in coming out. In these cases the now-adult children already have children of their own—your grandchildren. This may create sort of a double "whammy" for you in your journey.

Our children frequently, as adults, have become as much our peers, colleagues and advisors as they have remained our children. Now we are threatened by the possible betrayal of all these roles our children have grown into over their adult years.

Depending on how your adult children receive this news about being gay, your relationship with your grandchildren may well be affected. In most family situations, the parents (your children) will probably want to control the flow of information about your lifestyle. As long as the children are young, this request, if made, should be respected. In the event your children want you to take responsibility for explaining your coming out to your grandchildren, proceed much in the same way that has already been outlined in other parts of this book.

Grandparents frequently occupy special places in the eyes of their "grandkids." They are viewed as the extra nurturer, the one person who can be depended upon when the grandchild needs that extra quarter he could not manage to squeeze out of his allowance or Dad. You may be revered as the keeper of extra wisdom and knowledge and surely have long since given up the carnal and venal things of life—especially sexual identity and, of course, sex.

As in all parts of the book, we encourage real relationships, telling the truth about yourself and your relationships, thereby setting up boundaries around relationships that are honest and trustworthy. Keeping with the truth creates trust and, better yet, it leaves you with only one story about yourself—the real one.

The following case history took place over almost three years in its development. Its narrative will part in format from the text of the book in an effort to demonstrate how one family comes to grips with a gay father and a gay son coming out at approximately the same time. It further demonstrates how far reaching the effects of a change in lifestyle can be in a single family and how many relationships must be rearranged as these individuals get centered with their real selves.

**Case Study**

Frank and Marion had been married for 30 years. Theirs had been a model marriage, relationship and family. Frank met Marion in grade school. Their playground romps matured into sweetheart dating and later serious dating that turned into a double graduation surprise. Both graduated with honors, her valedictorian and him salutatorian. After giving their respective honors speeches, they announced their engagement to be married within the month. Since everyone expected the childhood couple to remain a couple, the announcement came as a surprise to no one.

Over the ensuing years, Frank and Marion continued to be the model couple, relationship and then parents. In rather rapid succession they had added five children to the family rolls. The joke around town was Marion must have married pregnant and just decided to stay that way.

Frank provided a good living for his family. He became a successful CPA, deacon of the church, president of the Rotary Club and Senior Scoutmaster in the town. Marion was equally civic. Appearing to be a tireless mother and wife, her children were always immaculate in appearance, punctual and polite. She was an accomplished piano instructor, played for the church, taught Sunday school and was the president of the PTA for many years.

The children had arrived like stairsteps. Frank Jr. was followed by a brother or sister every year — Marianne, Josh, Jack and Suzann. Being so close in age, the children became their own best friends. All appeared to have followed the correct formula of good manners, mixed with enough harmless mischievousness to be collectively know as the *Lil' Rascals*.

The Rascals followed very much in their parents footsteps, all fairly well accomplished in academia, sports and community events.

As the children became less *Rascals* and more adults, they began to find people to date and with whom to develop serious relationships. After the usual years of mixed up, teen puppy-loves, all appeared to become seriously attached rather rapidly, except Josh who remained mostly a loner.

Frank Jr., later just Junior, being more like his father than the other boys, also became serious with the girl he was dating during his high school years. His father thought they were spending too much time together and perhaps getting too serious. Junior delighted in throwing his father's history up to him, frequently citing his "17½, can't wait until I'm 18 to get married." During their more serious tag team conversations about the virtues and responsibilities of dating, Junior would kiddingly say, "Why was I born just seven months after you and Mom got married? Did y'all do it before you got married?" Frank always interrupted with the same patent answer, "Junior, you know all you children came early (which for the most part was true). You were too young to realize, but Suzann was so early we almost lost her. That's why we stopped trying to have kids . . . well, one of the reasons . . . you just turned out to be bigger and tougher than the others."

That was the first time Frank had used the bigger—

always tougher—but never bigger. Being egged on by his developing teen curiosity, Junior decided to look for his birth certificate in his father's filing cabinet. Everyone had been admonished to stay out of the files, as Frank kept some of his client account folders in there and these were confidential. Wanting to respect his father's wishes, Junior knew these files were probably the ones marked "private and confidential," so he would not invade those.

Picking a Sunday afternoon when the family would be away for hours and he would be home alone "wooing his lush," as Suzann put it, provided the perfect opportunity to look into the private domain and see what secrets were held about his birth. Junior's search had just begun when he saw a folder marked "birth certificates." He quickly found his and after dwelling on the pomp of the parchment and legal seals, his eyes focused on the date of birth. To his amazement, while at the same time less of a surprise than he had anticipated, he had been born six months to the day after their marriage. Then the big shocker—weight nine pounds, 12 ounces—hardly premature. In his own broadminded way he chuckled, "So I was in the oven before the baker said 'I do!' "

Putting aside this passing confirmation of a seldom thought-on possibility, Junior carefully replaced the folder and closed the file. Since curiosity fostered this search and since curiosity was still alive and well, *and* since there was still plenty of time before anyone came home, he decided to take a quick glance at a confidential file. Taking a few folders out simultaneously, making sure to note their exact location and keeping them in alphabetical order, Junior scanned the first few. There seemed to be nothing unusual about the contents. Names, addresses, age, a few hardly legible notes detailing times, dates, lunch meetings and the like. Since he had never looked at a CPA's files, he was unsure of what to look for and became somewhat upset at himself for prying. After thumbing through a few more files and making sure they were in their original order, Junior began to notice a curious common factor in the folders. All of these clients were men and each folder contained a picture of the client signed with some benign endearment and their names. As he was putting these away, he recalled seeing some of these men with his father and just assumed these were friends of his parents and the picture had been sent with a holiday card. It would be a number of years before Junior really discovered the significance of these files.

Junior had been wanting to get more serious with his current girlfriend, perhaps even have sex if the opportunity presented itself. His parents had been dutiful in supplying all the kids with good sex education and parenting information. He anticipated his parents' response if he brought it up, but now, armed with his new found information, he felt he would have the perfect defense and rationale.

It was not too long before this defense was put to the test. Just turned 17-years-old and really feeling his manhood, Junior decided his best birthday present would be from his longtime girlfriend, Debra. Not having thought ahead for this event, neither he nor Debra provided any contraception for the event, justifying it by thinking, "No one gets pregnant the first time . . ."

About six weeks later Junior received a panic call from Debra. She was two weeks late for her period. There was some fleeting thought of a quickie pregnancy test and possibly an abortion, but that was soon replaced by a more calm attitude and decision to go to their parents and get some advice.

Both sets of parents took the news rather well. They went through the usual admonitions of "this could ruin your chances for a good education, career, etc." and the more trying, "what will the neighbors think, etc." Junior and Deb had rehearsed this part of the encounter and decided to take control by saying to his father, "Look, Dad, you've not done so bad for yourself. You married Mom just after you turned 18, and I know Mom already was pregnant. You may be mad at me and have a right to be, but I looked in your files (Junior noted a strange pallor on his father's face) and saw my birth certificate. I could not have been three months premature and weigh over nine pounds (again Junior noted a strange sigh of relief when he mentioned only the birth certificate).

Frank, in a deeper voice than usual, chuckled, "Well,

like father, like son. What can I say? You've just decided
to be a man a few years early. Now, of course, we expect
you to do what is right by Debra. We'll back whatever responsible decision you two make. Now, with a bit of un-
easiness in his voice, he went on, "And about the files.
You certainly have a right, son, to look at files that affect
you or belong to you. I should have kept those papers
where you could get to them any time you needed. I also
appreciate you respecting the confidentiality of the client files." Pausing more like he was asking if Junior had
looked at them and wanting to be assured that he had
not, he rambled on in a nervous, concocted southern
drawl. "Gee, no telling what you might think if you read
them. Might think that my little black book was full of
all the cute numbers I've been having affairs with. Miss
Smith (a name he fabricated out of the air) would faint
if she thought someone saw her files. Crooked as a dog's
hind leg, she is!"

Junior passed this overly solicitous explanation with
little thought. It once again crossed his mind that he
had seen only men in the file with their pictures and no
accounting types of records. However, he had not
looked through very many of them and "S" for Smith
would have been deep in the cabinet. He chuckled to
himself, "Dad—affair?—no way. Besides, they were
mostly men and of all the AC-DC men he had known in
his life, Dad was strictly AC!"

These thoughts as well as his original curiosity at
viewing the files was not to come into his awareness
again for a number of years.

Life went on without much great drama. Junior, like
his father, immediately attempted to populate the
earth. He and Debra had a child almost yearly and two
sets of twins. He completed school and college and
worked at first part-time, then full time for his father.
His children thought their grandpa hung the moon
and invented apple pie. Frank was the ideal grandparent—present, attentive, perhaps a bit too generous.

The other children, in similar manner, were beginning their own successful adult stories. Marianne married early, too, at 19. She was rather involved in the
"plan and limit your family" movement. She decided on

two pregnancies, two children. One pregnancy, one child. Surprise! Second pregnancy, triplets. She laughingly blamed it on Junior, saying he started this multiple birth business.

Josh and Jack were slow to date. While involved in the usual growing up activities, they both became quite studious in college with plans for careers in medicine. Jack married a fellow student during medical school. Josh never married.

Suzann stayed home the longest. She went through a short marriage that ended tragically with her husband's death in the waning days of the Vietnam war. Ray, her husband, never saw their only daughter. While Suzann had a home of her own, she stayed at her parent's house frequently, stating she needed to help her Mom since Dad's business had grown so big and he had to be away over night more and more in recent years.

Nearing their thirtieth anniversary, Marion felt her marriage slipping. She made many excuses for the change. In fact, her most frequent reason for the change was just that, "THE CHANGE." After all, it was that time of life for her and she had many of the characteristic signs—mood swings, hot flashes and some weight gain. Marion believed that men go through a sort of menopause, too. Frank Sr. had become a little more moody, less affectionate, much less interested in sex. Then she would "pooh pooh" the whole notion of life changes and growing older. The most probable cause was Frank's businesses. They had grown much more than anyone had expected. He had diversified into a large CPA consulting firm, handling many important accounts, and recently had bought a real estate franchise. His frequent out-of-town trips with overnight and weekend absences were to be expected. Marion almost single-handedly managed the real estate franchise.

Thinking all of this through a second time, Marion decided they were old enough and successful enough to slow down and let the businesses run themselves. Suzann needed something to do to snap her out of her loss —enough years had passed since Ray's death. Marion decided to groom her for the real estate business. Junior certainly knew his father's business and should be taking on more responsibility.

Realizing how well she was handling this marital slowdown, Marion decided to do some reading about spicing up their marriage. Frank Sr. had already joined a health club and since it was for men only, she was unable to accompany him to work out. That was just as well because they were so competitive at times they would probably wear each other out seeing who could swim the most laps. Marion called her neighbor, who belonged to a spa, and asked if she could take her up on the one month free trial membership. Betty had been after her for months to go to the spa with her and was delighted to accommodate the request.

During the first few days, Marion complained about her various aches and pains from being a novice athlete. She told Betty how Frank unmercifully teased her while applauding her efforts. Betty said, "Why don't you show him? If you buy a membership here you can get one for your spouse free for an entire year. Or, if you are not ready to buy yet, he can come in on my husband's membership for a free month."

Marion enthusiastically and a bit boastfully replied, "Oh, Frank has belonged to a spa for years. You've seen how trim he is. Always so tanned and stylish, you'd think he was going on 30 instead of 50."

Betty, in her half-serious half-joking way, asked, "Why don't you go to that spa, or would the competition be too great? You two are such a team!"

Marion responded, equally joking, "That would be swell, but I would want to go alone. You see, it's a men-only spa, so I can't. Isn't that just my luck? All that flesh just going to waste without us girls there to drool over it!"

Betty, asking in a non-invasive fashion, said "That's strange. I thought all spas had to be co-ed—same but equal, you know—that N.O.W. stuff. Are you sure they don't just have one day for men and alternating days for women? What is the name of it?"

Realizing that she had never given this spa much thought, Marion said, "I don't know that he's ever mentioned the name. He just says "the club" and come to think of it, I've never seen a check or receipt for the fees. And he is always so careful with his bookkeeping. Oh, well, no big deal. It has certainly kept him in shape!"

Almost apologetically Betty replied in a slightly muted tone, "The only health spa or club I know of downtown is a gay bath and everyone calls it "the club." Then, with a dramatic change in tone and style, Betty continues, "Would you just listen to us! We sound like we're the over-the-hill gang, looking for something to gossip about. We're the ones who should worry about our shapes. Who knows, both our husbands may start to look at the boys." Both laughed these thoughts off as they continued the day in other pursuits.

While thumbing through a family type magazine in the spa waiting room, Marion noted an ad for a marriage renewal weekend. Several of the symptoms of the *Is Your Marriage In Trouble* checklist matched many of the things Marion was noticing in her marriage—a seemingly absent partner even when he or she is present, decreased and more meaningless conversation, little or no sex, increased time away from home and many others. The promised outcome was an improvement in all of these areas as well as a "refreshing new honesty in your partner and yourself."

Quite excited about her new found direction, Marion filled out the application and wrote a check for her and Frank's registration. Tonight she would ask for his attendance at this weekend retreat for her thirtieth anniversary gift. As coincidence would have it, the Saturday night of the first full weekend day was the date on which they were married. She began to romanticize this as the start of a second marriage and envisioned it as possible second honeymoon.

That evening she presented the proposal to him. He could not have been more delighted. In fact, he had been thinking along the same lines of personal growth. "Gee, great minds run in the same channels. I've just signed up for a thing called the Advocate Experience," Frank informed her. He went on the explain, "It is a weekend of very intense, executive-type training to make you a better advocate of your own product, which I understand is yourself. This might have been a good course for you since you are now in the real estate end of our business, but enrollment is limited and already closed."

Sounding delighted, Marion responded, "Thank goodness. I thought we were getting sluggish, having spent so much time together. You should have heard Betty and I today at the mall. We were carrying on like a soap opera. So foolish . . ." she trailed off in the other room finishing her statements without Frank being able to hear her.

Early that Friday morning, Frank left for his Advocate Experience weekend. Marion busied herself about the house getting things ready for the following weekend of marital renewal. Betty called inviting them over for supper and sort of a pre-anniversary party. Marion said, "Oh, in all the excitement I forgot to tell you Frank is attending an executive training of some sort. Sounds kind of strange because it is supposed to be very deep and very personal so that they cannot talk about it until it is all over, then they can tell only their experience. Oh well, welcome to the executive world."

Only half listening to this narrative, Betty said, "Could we have a raincheck or maybe do something Wednesday?"

"Gee, thanks," Marion responded. "Wouldn't you know, we spend months with nothing to do but sit at home and watch television. Now we're covered up with invitations."

"Guess you'll have to get you a social secretary!" Betty retorted in a fun-filled pseudosophisticated tone. "What in the world do you do on Wednesday night?"

"Nothing usually, but this Wednesday Frank has his after-meeting or post-meeting or something. Everyone who does the weekend has to attend it." Marion answered.

"That's strange for a meeting night with all the church services and such. What is the name of this thing?" Betty inquired.

"Advocate Experiences, I think," Marion replied, trying to recall the exact name.

"You mean The Advocate Experience," Betty quickly interjected. "There is something strange here. Sean (her eldest son) began having some questions about his sexuality after a few brief gay encounters at college. I encouraged him to see a counselor at the college. This is just a stage all boys go through and Sean is just a little late. The counselor advised him to go to the weekend encounter but it is supposed to help people who have questions or issues regarding homosexuality. They also have a post-meeting the following Wednesday. Oh, listen to us rambling on like last week. I'm sure it is a coincidence or maybe Frank has someone gay working for him and he wants to understand them, I mean the gays, better."

Somewhat less enthused Marion said, "I'm sure you're right." She then continued her preparations for the next weekend.

Frank's weekend came and went. In keeping his pact with the group from the weekend, he told Marion he could not discuss it until after Wednesday. When Wednesday arrived, Frank had an out-of-town meeting and would return just in time for their renewal weekend. Just before leaving on the Wednesday closure meeting for the weekend experience, Frank gave Marion an unusually large diamond ring as an early anniversary gift and took a little trip to the bedroom for an afternoon filled with passion that Marion had not experienced in years. On his way out the door, Frank said, "Just remember, *that* and diamonds are forever. See ya' Friday, gorgeous!"

Marion was more enthused and excited than ever. She called Betty and flooded her with the excitement and news. Betty's voice remained rather staid and sullen. Marion inquired if there was anything wrong, but Betty responded blandly that nothing was wrong and wished Marion and Frank a happy and informative weekend.

While continuing preparations for the weekend, Marion noticed several suits and other pieces of clothing missing from Frank's wardrobe. The file also was gone. Frank had been discussing setting up a small efficiency apartment for out-of-town clients. He probably was setting up a temporary office to facilitate those clients and kept a change or two of clothes there for emergencies. Marion always had a way of justifying these strange, little unexplained events.

Friday came and like clockwork Frank appeared, ready to go. Marion was packed and they embarked on their four-hour journey to the renewal retreat. Marion thought this would be the perfect time to share about the weekend. However, Frank cautioned against it, saying, "It will be best for the process to start before we can go for it."

Marion curiously responded, "It . . . process . . . what is this, a new hip language or something?"

"No," he laughed. "Before tomorrow is over you will be using the same language!"

The remainder of the trip was spent in a quiet but slightly awkward fashion. All serious subjects were off limits. Even the surprisingly delightful diamond and "roll in the hay" now seemed far away.

Saturday went well. Marion got in the mood of the event. She could not remember so much laughter or so many tears, some happy, some sad, even some still bitter over Suzann's loss because of Vietnam. She felt a soul cleansing of sorts and a safety about asking Frank anything, no, ANYTHING, *NO, ANYTHING*. She felt so free; if a person had to wait until their thirtieth anniversary, the rewards were well worth it.

From eight that night on was alone/together time. That is, it was a time to be alone with one another together in the relationship. No outside plans, no socializing with other couples, no being alone/alone. What wonderful rules, Marion thought. That way no one could have excuses not to be with their relationship.

The first place Marion wanted to start was to remark on that Wednesday afternoon, the one with the roll in the hay and the emergence of this new Frank. She began by reinforcing her excitement and pleasure. "Frank, I almost felt like I was having an affair with a new person. You haven't acted like that in 20 years. Promise me that new person won't ever hide again. I . . ."

Politely interrupting, Frank replied, "Marion, in a way a new person *was* there. Granted, it was me but there is a part of me that has been buried most of my life. Using the vernacular, in the closet, so to speak. I've discovered that's right on, calling it in the closet. That is how I've felt, especially for the last few years. And I think it is safe to say that part of me won't go away again. After the discoveries I made about myself, you, us, the kids . . . I can't believe how different I feel about everything. It's such a freedom, such a new-found freedom, that I just had to share the joys of it with the most important person in my life!"

Feeling even more complete, Marion interrupted to try and clear up some encroaching confusion, "You remember Sean, Betty's kid? Well, he went to a meeting similar to yours. Seems like the poor child was having some identity crisis because of a homosexual experience or two while in college. I can't imagine being so upset over something all boys go through at some point in their life. It's just a phase . . . making it necessary to go through an entire weekend trying to figure it out. I told Betty . . ."

"I saw Sean there," Frank interrupted more briskly. "He sure was surprised to see me, but I can't say I was surprised to see him."

"That's just what I told Betty," Marion said, sounding increasingly nervous. "I said I wasn't sure why you'd be going unless you had a gay employee and were trying to understand them better . . ."

"Us better," interjected Frank. "Us . . ."

"Like I told Betty, Sean was thinking about going to work for you . . . nice of you to go out of your way for them!" Marion proceeded as if she had not heard Frank's words.

Firmly Frank said, "Marion, I said understand US, not them. I went to the weekend to understand my sexuality. It was a coincidence that I saw Sean, but no surprise. My being there was for me and had nothing to do with Sean."

Now fighting back tears, Marion gasped, "I can't believe what I'm hearing. You can't be . . . you know . . . that way! You're married and so masculine. I mean, just look at last Wednesday afternoon. Sean, I mean, I can understand Sean, well, at least a little. He is sort of delicate and sensitive. But you, you're . . ."

Trying to reassure and clarify at the same time, Frank replied, "Marion, most gays are not as you are trying to describe or believe. You cannot tell us from anyone else, unless we let you know. The stereotype you are familiar with is more a product of the media than real life. Being gay does not impair my sexual performance. There are more parts to being gay than just the sex stuff. As a matter of fact, at least for me, that is the least important part. I don't expect you to even begin to understand all of this in one day. It is going to take time."

Continuing in half panic and half shock, Marion pleaded, "But what about the kids. Junior just idolizes you. Suzann has never gotten over Ray's death, now this. It would be like losing her Dad! Jack will just die. You know how he talks about hating queers, I mean gays. And the grandkids . . . how will . . ."

Again trying to take control, Frank said, "You just worry about you. I've arranged to take off for the next few days. Junior is capable of running everything. We are going to sort all of this out together."

Still worrying, Marion asked, "But what will you tell them?"

Frank firmly replied, "The truth!"

For the next few days Marion and Frank spent countless hours sorting out 30 years together, 30 years during which an important part of Frank's life had been closeted. Marion started with the most recent events Betty seemed to have picked up on that were not at all obvious to Marion. Part of her questioning seemed to surface as a morbid curiosity, some answers she was afraid to hear, but she dearly wanted to understand this complex part of the man she loved so deeply.

She discovered "the club" was indeed the gay baths Betty knew about. Frank admitted going there to work out and occasionally for sex. The files were actually men he had known over the years, both as gay friends and some as sex partners. He explained the apartment was indeed for their out-of-town clients, but until they needed to use it, he had moved some of his clothes and files there . . . not knowing how Marion would react to his coming out. He told her she had every right to be angry and order him out of the house. Therefore, he just wanted to be prepared until things could be worked out.

The more they shared, the more Marion understood. She felt a special closeness because of Frank's trust in her for coming out and her earlier disappointment and sense of betrayal began to subside. Towards the end of their unscheduled sabbatical, Marion felt more adjusted to the news and decided she and Frank could work things out as they had always done. Once more her attention turned towards the kids. She wanted to show a united front and delay telling the kids as long as possible.

On their return home, nothing seemed out of the ordinary. The entire clan met over at Frank and Marion's house . . . home to everyone in the family. Junior was busy updating Dad on the business. All of the grandkids were rummaging through the souvenir gifts and crawling on Grandpa, each struggling for their turn riding piggyback. Suzann and Josh were off to their usual partial seclusion as had been the case ever since Ray was killed. Marion would find herself fighting back tears, realizing things might never be just like this again. Frank appeared to be immersed in the spirit of the homecoming.

As the day was growing late, everyone started to leave. Junior told Frank just to let him know if he needed more time, there was no reason to rush back to the office. Thanking him for the gesture, Frank jokingly let him know he would be there bright and early, because "the old man is not out of the saddle yet!" Suzann and Josh had remained in the game room away from the rest of the family. Marion came in asking, "Am I interrupting anything? Is there something wrong?"

On her exit from the room Suzann said, "Nothing out of the ordinary for this family. Say good-bye to Dad. In a hurry, you know."

Josh, now alone with Marion, said, "What a day! All of this excitement and rushing around, almost seems like Christmas."

"Yes, it does," Marion endorsed. "Too bad you haven't settled down yet and started your family. During these get-togethers you are always the first one to leave. Anything unusual about today?"

Mustering up his courage, Josh said, "I've been needing to have a talk with you, actually both of you, but with the recent turn of events, I guess just you."

A flashback fear leaped into Marion's throat, assuming Josh knew something about Frank, perhaps from Sean. She thought maybe Sean told him about seeing Frank at the weekend. Taking a deep breath, Marion asked, "Is this something about your father?"

"Not directly, no, but in a way, yes. It's all sort of confused right now," Josh replied.

"I guess you know your father recently attended one of those growth seminars, like EST," Marion offered, fishing for what Josh already knew.

"Yeah, I know he was there. The seminar was the Advocate Experience Weekend. It is for gays mostly or people with issues regarding homosexuality," Josh clarified.

Surprised at the information, Marion was a little irritated that Sean had been out telling everyone who he had seen at the seminar. Wondering how much information was out in the neighborhood, Marion asked, "Oh, did Sean tell you?"

Since a part of the agreement at the weekend is confidentiality, Josh was upset that perhaps Frank had told Marion about Sean's attendance, thus breaking the spirit of the agreement. With equal irritation Josh added, "How did you know Sean was there? Did Dad tell you?"

With some surprise at Josh's irritation, Marion answered, "Heavens no. Betty told me Sean's college counselor advised him to go, so when Frank was telling me about his experience, I just naturally mentioned Sean . . ."

"Wait a minute," Josh interrupted, realizing some misinformation was being perpetuated, "I'm the 'counselor' who told Sean to go. We just made up that other bit because I wasn't ready to tell you and, well, you know how long a secret lasts between you and Betty. I told Sean to go. I was one of those guys with whom Sean had an experience. I went there basically to get some support in coming out to you and Dad. I had no idea Dad would be there. I was going to tell you both anyway, but now Dad already knows at least what I had to say to the group. Mom, something happened there, something special that I can't really explain. Something special between me and Dad. I feel I met a part of him that he has been hiding." Starting to feel tears well up inside, he continued, "Mom, there was this exercise we had to do where you just go around and hug everyone in the room while looking them in the eyes. I was very nervous when I came to Dad. But I reached out to hug him and for the first time in my life I felt all of him was there and in a way I felt all of me was there. Mom, we just hung on to each other and cried like two babies as if we had been separated for a hundred years. Oh Mom, it was great. I never want to lose that great feeling . . ." unable to complete his thoughts for the tears, Josh stood there weeping openly.

Marion, deeply moved and shedding her own tears, was able to say between gasps, "Yes, dear, I know what you mean, I know what you mean. I, too, experienced that completeness in your father, and it did feel very good. I'm just so afraid that all of this complete stuff will come between us . . ." and Marion, also unable to go on, just held Josh and they cried, realizing an understanding of what had just happened and all of its implications that were beyond words.

The following morning, true to his word, Frank showed up at the office bright and early. He was a bit nervous because he had chosen this day to come out to Junior. His mind was going wild because Junior was more or less his clone. They looked alike, talked alike, frequently even dressed alike. Frank harbored a secret fear . . . "what if Junior was also like him . . . i.e., gay." How would he deal with that? Frank all along had his own suspicions about Josh. No girl friends, very studious, overly private about his social life. Except for Sean, they really did not know any of his friends. Trying to avoid driving himself crazy, Frank would remember his agreement from the weekend seminar. BE HERE NOW. That is just what he planned to do . . . deal with his coming out to Junior and let the rest deal with itself. When Junior arrived and the usual morning amenities were out of the way, Frank approached Junior saying, "Been meaning to have a talk with you and this seems to be as good a time as any. You've handled this business just as I would while we were away and I feel you could continue if I needed to be away for awhile."

"Sure," Junior interjected. "You deserve a rest. Hell, take a cruise, go around the world. You and Mom have worked hard. Enjoy your money."

"Wait, you don't quite understand," Frank clarified. "I need to get away and do some serious thinking—alone."

"Oh, tired of the old bat, huh? Need to get away so it's just you and the boys!" Junior quipped.

Trying to keep on a serious note, Frank said, "I know you mean well . . . and you are closer than you think. No, I'm not really tired of the old bat (chuckling) as you put it, but I may need to spend some more time with the boys, that is after I've had time alone to sort through some things."

"You and Mom aren't having any problems, are you?" Junior inquired.

"Not in the way you might think," Frank answered. "I love your mother very much. We've raised quite a family, built a good business, stuck it out through thick and thin for over 30 years. However, there is a part of me that I've kept hidden from everyone, maybe even myself, until recently. Your quip about spending more time with the boys is more on target than you probably know. You see, son, I'm . . . well, you know, either bisexual or gay. I've really not sorted it all out myself. That's why I need the time away."

With a great deal of astonishment and denial, Junior responded, "Dad, you've told some flat jokes in your days, but this stinks. What's the punch line . . . Dad goes gay after fathering five children, married 30 years, grandparent, civic leader . . . damn! Sounds like something from one of those rag tabloids. Have you tried this one on Mom yet? She'll get the biggest laugh."

Trying to gain control of Junior's histrionics, Frank said, "As bad as some of my jokes have been, this is not one of them. There is no punch line. I am what I am, now I just have to figure out how I fit into the picture here, with this . . . I mean, my family."

Now more somber, Junior replied, "God! I don't know what to say. What you must think of me with all my queer jokes. Well, are you going to tell Mom?"

Feeling some relief at Junior's seriousness, Frank responded, "In the first place, Jack has you championed with the queer jokes, and I've always thought them funny and still do. I do not take them as a reflection on me. In the second place, I've already told your Mother. For now most everything is on hold. She felt, and I agreed, that I needed to clear things with myself and you kids before we make any dramatic decisions about us."

"Leave it to Mom to take care of everyone else first!" Junior retorted.

The remainder of the day was spent filling in the pieces. Frank brought up the filing cabinet that Junior had looked into for his birth certificate. Junior admitted having seen the folders with accounts of only men and the pictures. He reported having a fleeting thought about the possibility of Dad being gay, but discounted it as absurd and crazed teenage thinking and really hadn't given it a second thought.

Frank discussed the insights he gained during the weekend and the marriage renewal. He appreciated integrating all the truths about himself, which brought up the subject of the grandchildren. It was at this juncture that Frank admitted being in therapy for about a year, just trying to get to this place in his life. He related the feelings of the therapist that true psychological health and comfort comes from working towards complete integration of all the parts of one's whole self, even those parts we would rather dismiss.

Meanwhile Josh, feeling incomplete about yesterday's discussion with his mother, returned to the house hoping Frank would be there, too. When he arrived he could tell Mom was still in a state of indecision, somewhat overwhelmed by so much shocking information in such a short time. Once again Mom was worried about how this was going to effect everyone else. Before Josh could get into much of what he had to say, Marion asked, "What in the world is going to happen to this family? Poor Suzann. This will be like another death to her. You have more or less taken Ray's place since he died. You both have become so close over the last few years."

Josh interrupted her worried delivery. "Please don't try to fix this thing over night. Just concentrate on taking care of yourself. In the first place, Suzann has known for years. She was the first one I told. I was worried about the draft, especially after Ray was sent to 'Nam. Not that I was afraid to serve my country, but rather afraid of being found out in the army and either getting a dishonorable discharge or put up with a lot of harassment. Suzann is more responsible for me pursuing a medical career than my real interest. She, Ray and I discussed the situation and he said the word in 'Nam was if you are unmarried, you'd better be in college, especially pre-med or med school, and they'd leave you alone. So there you have it—become a doctor to avoid discrimination. I always teased Suzann . . . if she ever got tired of Ray, I got him. In fact, we were chuckling over a letter he wrote to Suz and his spare, meaning me, when the black telegram came. I so remember her being there for me when I first came out, feeling so alone and scared. It was as though a part of both of us died when we read the news. That experience sort of fused us together."

Appearing somewhat relieved at one less person's feelings to take care of, Marion replied, "How could all of this be going on with me being unaware? I'm not exactly naive, you know. None of you look or act gay!"

"Mom, we don't run around with a big 'H' on our forehead. There are millions of us and we are your neighbors, friends, children and even sometimes husband," Josh replied, trying to broaden Mom's understanding.

"How have you and your Father worked this out?" Marion inquired.

"Well, for the most part, we have not discussed it. The way the weekend was designed, we responded to and through the group, more than to each other. We have a lot to say. I was so very afraid of how Dad would react. I just knew he would scream and yell and order me out of the house. I should have known better. Dad is not that sort. I'm sure he is wondering the same thing about my reaction. I wanted what I got from him at the weekend, that complete feeling, you know." Josh replied.

About that time Frank came home to tell Marion he would be away for a few days. He saw Josh and asked, "Where do I go from here?"

Josh shrugged his shoulders and they embraced again, with tears streaming down their cheeks. Then Frank added, "Why does one part of me feel so free and complete and the other so full of fear and empty?"

Still holding on, Josh replied, "I don't know Dad. I just believe what we learned at the weekend, and you will absolutely know when you get "it." So go for "it" and let us know when you have arrived.

While Frank was away, nothing was said about his situation to the other family members. Josh made his rounds of coming out to the rest of the family. Everyone was rather accepting, most saying we still love you, there is nothing different today than before. Don't worry about it. Marianne had some reservations about his telling Dad since he was so socially conscious about the family. Josh told her he already knew and did okay with the information. However, now Josh was worried about Marianne's reception of the same news from Dad.

When Frank returned he had his mind made up. He would call all of his kids together and come out, hoping the support he already had would help him over any rough spots.

Since he and Josh had not had the time to discuss their mutual areas of coming out and to whom this has been done, Frank felt he owed Josh the courtesy of a call, letting him in on his plan. Josh let his Dad know he had already come out to his brothers and sisters. Everything had gone rather smoothly. It was a mutual decision not to discuss any of this with the grandchildren due to their young ages.

Frank called all of the children to arrange a meeting at his house. He asked all to arrange for sitters since he, following Josh's lead, did not know how to approach any questions that might be asked by young children.

There was a strange ambience in the house as the family began to arrive. Since Frank had always considered his children's spouses as his own kids, he insisted they be a part of this. Frank commented to Marion that this was almost like a funeral, everything seeming so somber. Marion returned the comment with, "I suppose it is a funeral of sorts. A part of this family will be buried today."

Josh and Junior already knew what part of today's agenda would be. Both in their own way also were fearing that a divorce might be announced. While neither had great difficulty in accepting that their father was gay, neither could envision their parents being apart. The thought of Marion remarrying and Dad taking on a gay lover was almost incomprehensible, even for Josh. During his drive over to the house, Josh wrestled with his feelings regarding this very component of his father's journey to come out and be comfortable as a gay person. He almost wished for another Advocate weekend to prepare him for the loss of a parental unit he had known all life. He almost felt like a traitor to his father's cause . . . he himself was gay and at the same time he was holding on to wanting nothing to change between his parents. This created a most disturbing paradox.

With everyone in attendance, Frank appeared in the living room. Looking drawn and tired, and maybe for the first showing his age, he cleared his throat and began, "I realize some of you kids know why I've called you all together, and some are in the dark. First let me clear the air by saying there is nothing terribly wrong between your Mother and me. Neither of us has cancer or anything like that, so don't start trying to spend your inheritance yet." A nervous chuckle went through the living room. Frank always tried to bring a little levity into any discussion, no matter how grave. He felt a little relief after hearing the chuckle in the room, but found the next words would not come out so easily.

Marion nudged him gently, saying, "Take your time. Your family has always been able to work through anything. We can work through this."

Taking a deep breath and with an unfamiliar tremolo in his voice, Frank tried again. "For some strange reason I feel like I am the child and you are the parents, and I have a confession to make. Part of me feels ashamed and naughty and part of me is struggling to become whole. As you all know, over the past few weeks I have been going to some seminars. Actually they are a part of my therapy. It was a coincidence that your Mother planned the marriage renewal weekend. I am not sure what we renewed, but we sure became closer. During that night of the renewal weekend, I told your Mother that I think I am bisexual or maybe gay. I am still struggling with which . . ." Tears were now spilling down his cheeks and Marion just held his arm waiting for him to continue.

Josh was also having his own tears as was Suzann. This event brought back a lot they had already been through and each understood the difficulty of telling your loved ones your innermost secret while feeling more vulnerable than you've ever felt before. Josh choked out a barely audible, "We love you, Dad."

Frank felt a surge of warmth go through him when he heard those words from the one who probably most fully understood what he was going through. He could only lip a "Thank you, Josh, I love you, too."

Junior, also fighting the tears said, "Dad, you're still the captain of this ship."

Trying to regain his composure and throw a bit of humor into the tension of the moment, Frank chuckled through his tears, "Junior, if you dare say we'll have to rename the ship the HMS Queen Mary, I'll deck you one."

Now looking toward Marion, Frank continued, "Well, I guess it is out now. I am neither more nor less of what I used to be. I still have some thinking through to do for myself. I don't really know enough about this sexuality stuff to give you any real answers . . . why I am this way, what causes it, why now at this stage of my life instead of earlier, or anything. However, my therapist has offered to spend some time with the entire family to answer any questions as best as he can."

Until the family could consult with the therapist, everyone decided it best not to tell any details to the grandchildren. While Frank insisted on finding out the proper things to say considering the varying ages of the grandchildren, he was firm about his commitment to telling the truth about himself. Since Josh had been out to Suzann for a number of years and would take his gay friends to her house for visits and dinners, her daughter, now nine, knew in her own way about Josh. Even so, nothing had ever been formally explained to her.

Frank's children had the usual plethora of questions. Was he born this way? How could he be interested enough in Marion to father five children? Most of the children had some notion that their preconceptions of homosexuality were based on media hype and stereotypes. However, it was very difficult for them to integrate this realism about their father.

The question of divorce repeatedly came up. There was a tremendous amount of anxiety on all the children's parts about that happening. Our advice to them was to let Frank and Marion decide that issue themselves. We certainly acknowledged that it would be very difficult for the family to process so much change, especially if a divorce happened in the near future. We discussed other cases in which a bisexual or gay parent chooses to remain married and just work out things as they occur. However, we did consider that to remain married simply for appearance sake would in all probability deteriorate a lot of the wonderful things Marion and Frank obviously had between them. We told the children the best they could do is to support their parents' decision about the continuation or disruption of their marriage.

Frank and Marion agreed with the children's decision to not tell the grandchildren anything as long as they decided to remain married. They did agree to honor Frank's request to tell the children the truth if they asked any questions. If Frank and Marion decided to dissolve their marriage, Frank agreed to take it upon himself to explain the situation to the grandchildren to the best of his ability. If he reached a stuck point, he would arrange to get the grandchildren into a children of gays group or take them to his therapist for assistance.

At the time we finished preparing this manuscript for publication, Marion and Frank had separated and were living in different residences. Little change had taken place in the business portion of their lives and they saw little need to discuss things with the children. Josh had found a lover and moved into a duplex he purchased after setting up his medical practice. Suzann moved into the opposite side and felt the need to have Josh come out to her daughter. In so doing, no questions were raised about Frank, and Josh, wishing to respect that part of his father's privacy, did not bring it up.

Over the past several years, we have not had contact with any of the family. We see Frank occasionally and he, too, has taken on a lover, but since he no longer is a client we have not asked any personal questions regarding his family.

We felt this case is exemplary in how complex this phenomenon of coming out can be. Just as this case had, the effects of coming out can be farther reaching than just your children or immediate family. We still hold to our conviction that it is your duty and responsibility to come out, if that be your choice.

# Legal Considerations

In this chapter on legal considerations we remind our readers that we are not attorneys nor do we present ourselves to be. Our legal references are drawn from general legal principles and cannot be applied to specific cases. Since laws vary from state to state, we include this chapter to stimulate you to think along legal lines and encourage you to confer with your personal attorney for specifics that involve you and your relationship. In preparing this chapter, we have consulted local attorneys and have relied heavily on the book, *A Legal Guide for Lesbian and Gay Couples* by Curry and Clifford (Nolo Press, 1980) We highly recommend its use for relationship planning whether or not your relationship included children.

In a previous chapter concerning your partner (specifically the non-parent partner), we outline three possible living arrangements and how they might impact children brought into the relationship and the relationship itself. Let's examine the relationship where both partners were in a co-parenting roles.

In Situation 1 we have three individuals, Roger, Mark his son, and his partner Max. Roger is the legal, therefore, the primary parent. Max wants to assume a co-parenting role after careful consideration and deliberation with Roger. It is essential to understand that Max has no legal claim as a parent on Mark, in spite of giving quality parenting time, emotional support and guidance, and even some or total financial support. To our knowledge, partners of the same sex cannot co-adopt a child; therefore, you could not adopt your partner's child unless he is willing to sever his parental rights to his child, the courts agree to the adoption, and there were no active challenges to the proceedings from other interested parties (grandparents, ex-spouses, relatives, even the state.[1] Since there is just one legal parent as far as the relationship goes, it is useful to enter into a co-parenting agreement with one another. Even with such arrangements the ex-spouse parent remains the other legal parent unless deceased or has relinquished his or her parental rights.

Co-parenting agreements need to include what parenting means to the relationship, including financial support, if any. There needs to be an agreement regarding issues of discipline, rewards, values, household rules, school, visits, sports, obligations for transportation, health care, etc. Any and everything your parents had to consider and do for you should be included in your parenting considerations for your child. It is obvious the major legal considerations for your child will be the responsibility of you—the primary parent. Using our earlier example of Roger and Max, there are times when the secondary parent—Max—will need to have some legal consideration regarding Mark. The most essential and pressing consideration is that of medical care. Under most state law, only Roger can give permission for routine (non-emergency) medical care. Roger's ex-wife can give consent in emergency situations. Max, having no legal relationship with Mark can give no permission routinely. In

---

[1]We had a case where one person, Bill, adopted his partner, Pat, and Pat's children. In this case Pat severed his parental rights to his children. This action made Bill the legal parent of Pat's children while Pat remained the natural parent and stayed in the home as Bill's adopted "child"/adult albeit partner. Because of the complex nature of this arrangement and its potential pitfalls, we do not recommend this procedure.

the case of a life and death emergency, no consent is required during the emergency for the doctor, hospital, or medical support system to render life saving care. This latter form of consent is implied by most state law. It is those non-life and death emergencies and routine care that we wish to address.

It is best for all parties concerned to have Roger assume responsibility for any form of consent when practical to obtain such consent. However, Roger will not always be readily available, nor are other relatives who might be able to give consent—non-minor brother or sister, grandparent, etc. In order to avoid this problem and delay in receiving consent for medical, surgical or dental treatment, guardianship papers can be drafted, spelling out the areas of consent Max can give when Roger is not available.

When preparing these documents they need to be clearly written—preferably typed—spelling out in detail the parameters of the consent, signed, witnessed and dated. A formal temporary guardianship needs to be notarized. Excellent examples of these forms are available in the book: *A Legal Guide for Lesbian and Gay Couples.* Many hospitals and emergency rooms have blank consent forms they will give you to take home and fill out and obtain the appropriate signatures. Included in that same document you can write in intentions for visiting privileges that would be the same for the primary parent. This does not guarantee the hospital, doctor or dentist will honor such a document, but they (the documents) have more weight than a vague document, and certainly no document is of no use. If you have concerns in this area, go to your local hospital, doctor, dentist or emergency care facility, and find out what type of consent forms they need in the event of such a case as described. Preplanning is the best rule of thumb.

Max may run into other less urgent reasons to have consenting authority or a temporary guardianship of Mark. There are multitudes of school activities that require parental consent—bus trips, sporting events, participation in pilot programs, etc. Many of these frequently arise on short notice and Roger may be unavailable. There also is the perpetual report card that needs a signature. As mentioned before, it is always best to have the signature of the primary parent if possible.

In cases of litigation involving your minor child there is no question regarding the parameters of consent. However, since routine parental consent for minors' activities seldom result in litigation, formal arrangements for the non-parent partner to convey parental consent is convenient and frequently wise. It also instills a greater sense of co-parenting and reduces the sense of "differentness" about the relationship.

In Max's situation as the non-parent partner, he has no legal obligation for Mark's financial support. He is free to contribute to his support in any amount he wishes or agrees to with Roger. Also, he may withdraw that financial support if he wishes with no obligation to continue beyond his own sense of fairness and duty. In the event of a support contract drawn up between Roger and Max, suit may be filed to enforce the contract, which would be a consideration at trial. However, beyond Max's willingness to abide by the contract, it is unlikely to be enforced beyond the date Max wishes to be relieved of those obligations.

This is vastly different than child support originating by court order, which is legally binding and enforceable by the judicial system, regardless of the circumstances of the relationship. Child support orders can be renegotiated, but only with the involvement of the two parties and the court giving the order. Even new agreements between consenting ex-spouses are not binding unless the court agrees, which is usually the case as long as it is in the best interests of the child.

Let's assume for a moment Roger and Max have raised, lived with and emotionally nurtured Mark from infancy through his tenth year. Roger is killed in an auto accident. Who takes care of Mark? Who is the parent? If Roger's ex-wife, Mary, is living, she would be recognized as the next of kin and rightful parent, unless she had relinquished her parental rights. Even so, in Mary's absence, surviving blood relatives would have a custodial claim and a strong case for Mark's custody. Even in the absence of any other custodial claims, rights of custody would not automatically fall to Max. It would be a decision left to the court.

A survivor's document, as a part of Roger's will, declaring Max the appointed foster parent and guardian of choice for Mark, will have some validity while other arrangements that are more legally binding are being made. Max has a good possibility of being made permanent foster parent or guardian of Mark, or he might even successfully adopt Mark, depending on the circumstances at the time.

Concerning the matter inheritance, since Max is not related to Mark, regardless of how long they lived in the same household, what kinds of financial and emotional contributions were made, and what undocumented intentions there may have been, Max would have no direct rights of survivorship and inheritance, based on a blood relationship, in the event of an estate left by Mark in the absence of a will. Likewise, there would be no rights of inheritance from Max to Mark in the absence of a will. This is another area we encourage you and your partner to pay attention to early in your relationship, as well as in your co-parenting situation.

In the other relationships we mentioned where the non-parent partner wants only a modified or no parenting role, legal considerations are still important, and worthy of the same interest given to Roger's and Max's relationship. They will serve to protect everyone's interest and make the relationship work more smoothly.

Since most of these cases will involve children from a previous heterosexual union, the non-custodial ex-spouse should be considered when planning these alternative arrangements. However, with the greater frequency of single parent adoptions and surrogate parenting, there will be more cases in which the second biological parent will not be a consideration for these co-parent plans.

If your choice is single parent adoption, there are several alternatives available to you. The least likely successful alternative is through a children's home or welfare agency if you want an infant. The demand for healthy infants is great and the numbers are small. Since the advent of birth control and greater acceptance and availability of abortion, the number of infants available for adoption is smaller yet. There may well be a bias against a single parent trying to adopt an infant through a welfare or adoption agency due to the large number of couples wishing to adopt an infant.

If your choice is through a public type agency, your best chances would be requesting a disabled, non-white, interracial or older child.

If you really want an infant, you would be more likely to be successful if you went through private channels or know of a woman who is pregnant and does not wish to parent the infant.

In all cases you do need a lawyer. In the majority of adoptions, your lifestyle will not be a plus. Great discretion is encouraged during the evaluation process, court proceedings and at the final adoption hearing. Co-parenting agreements should be negotiated after the adoption is final. However, the agreement to have or negotiate an agreement should be made before you ever embark on your adoptive search.

The case of artificial insemination and surrogate parenting gets more complex and simple at the same time. If you find a woman who is willing to bear a child and give it over for adoption at birth, there will be little difference in the final stages between that and regular adoption.

The simplicity of a case of artificial insemination lies in the fact there is a legal, biological bond established. This would involve a situation in which a gay male supplies his sperm to a female recipient with or without intercourse (see precautions contained in the chapter on AIDS).

While intercourse cancels the need for a third party, usually a physician for medically supervised artificial insemination, it may be an unwise choice if there is no desire to bond with the woman. Since attempts at impregnation may be multiple before pregnancy is achieved, there is latitude on both party's part to claim certain marital privileges, depending on state law, if the emotional state of one of the parties changed regarding the "technical" aspects of siring an offspring.

For artificial insemination, the donor sperm would be injected into the vaginal vault of the recipient female. This may or may not be done by a physician, depending on the donor and recipient's desire for medical supervision. Hopefully, this would be a mutual decision.

After pregnancy occurs, there is usually an agreement between the donor and recipient for the donor to pay for medical expenses, hospital and birthing costs and attorney's fees, if one is used. We do recommend using an attorney experienced in adoption, family law and surrogate parenting. Other fees paid would have to compensate the surrogate mother for time lost from work, etc, because there can be no fee involved that connoted you bought the baby, even if you did father the infant through artificial means. Babies are not for sale, nor should they be. We are aware of black-market babies. These are illegal, even worse they are abusive to the child, and we do not recommend that you engage that channel for the acquisition for a baby or child.

After the baby is born, if you are to be the sole legal parent of this child, the surrogate mother will have had to relinquish her parental rights. Since you have a legal, biologic relationship to the infant, there should be few problems. Again, we encourage you to use an attorney if you decide to go as far as to have the mother relinquish her parental rights. While the use of an attorney cannot absolutely prevent legal complications in the future, they can certainly decrease their likelihood.

If you are a lesbian able to bear children and desire to get pregnant, your situation will be somewhat less complex. You may wish to know the donor father or may choose to utilize semen from a sperm bank. If you know the donor father, the same procedure previously outlined would be encouraged. Repeated intercourse with the same man in order to get pregnant may give him ideas of marriage and/or certain rights accorded to marriage. Also, it will be necessary for him to relinquish his parental rights (and obligations) if you choose to be sole legal parent. The use of semen from a sperm bank will make the donor/father consideration unnecessary since these banks usually are set up to ensure anonymity. There is the possibility of using an intermediary between the father and recipient mother to provide some anonymity; however, this intermediary could succumb to pressures to reveal the identity of the recipient mother and/or donor father. The fewer the complexities of the arrangement, the better off for all concerned.

If the donor father and/or surrogate mother is known and traceable, there are certain issues of survivorship and inheritance that might need to be addressed. This may seem to be a premature consideration since you are just getting started with your family. However, if there are large amounts of property or financial considerations, and blood lines can be proved, things can get sticky. Remember how many "heirs" came out of the woodwork to stake a claim on the Howard Hughes estate. This is also a relatively new area in law so there are many test cases to be made. Your attorney can best advise you on these parameters should you decide the artificial insemination.

In the case of the donor gay father, no one can guarantee a healthy infant nor a reasonably inexpensive pregnancy. In the event of the birth of a deformed or seriously ill infant, someone has to pay the bill. The infant still needs the love and support of a parent. This specter looms over the head of this procedure in spite of the most careful planning and medical supervision. If you decide to try and pull out of the deal and paternity can be substantiated, you can be sued for and forced to pay child support. A case nationally televised on a popular talk show demonstrated how difficult the situation can get. As the case turned out, the donor father of the severely handicapped and retarded infant was not the donor father at all. Nevertheless, prior to knowing that, lawsuits were looming concerning responsibility for child care including a rather burdensome financial obligation. There was a tremendous display of moral indignation at the behavior of the parties in the case. Just imagine the outcry if one of the principles in such a dispute turns out to be gay or lesbian.

Similarly what was previously simpler for a lesbian wanting to get pregnant through the semen of a donor father, may turn out to be more complex in the event of complications at birth. In this case, it would be very difficult for the lesbian mother to disclaim responsibility at the birth of a severely disabled or seriously ill infant. After all, she is the one who was pregnant and gave birth. In the event of an anonymous semen donor, there would be almost no hope of creating co-responsibility with the donor father. In the event the donor father is known, at least there is a person against whom you may attempt some measure of liability, perhaps child support, but it would be difficult in the face of any liability exclusionary contracts. It would be beneficial to discuss these potential unfavorable consequences with your attorney before embarking on this project.

There are some gay men and lesbians who know each other, decide to conceive with the gay male being the donor father and the lesbian being the recipient mother, then making arrangements to share custody after the birth of the child.

In having counseled a number of gay and lesbian clients in adoption, artificial insemination and surrogate parenting, we have encountered a number of myths and misconceptions. Some men have believed that the very act of entering a contract with a surrogate mother, using his donor sperm, relinquished all of her parental rights at conception and the assumption of full, uncontested custody at birth was guaranteed. Not so. Parental (maternal) rights cannot be severed until after birth and in spite of agreements to the contrary, she can and may refuse to give up custody. That would entail pursuing another legal remedy entirely. If you choose some sort of litigation, you must consider that if your sexuality enters the legal argument, you are almost certain to lose.

Some women have stated motherhood is a fact, fatherhood is a rumor, and that is no less true for lesbian moms. Under that misconception some women have felt that they could use donor sperm from several known men or have intercourse with several men, then they (the men) could not claim paternity. Again, not so. The state of the art for paternity determination may still be a matter of being able to conclusively prove who the father is not rather than conclusively who the father is. However, with sophisticated state of the art tissue typing, the evidence can be so close as to convince a jury of paternity. Also, if the process of elimination is being utilized, and you had intercourse with only a limited number of men, conclusive exclusion by the process of elimination may yield paternity and the father.

We do not include these legal nightmares to scare prospective biological gay parents away from a scientific process and common medical procedure that can afford you parenthood and progeny. We do this to encourage everyone concerned to examine all the ramifications of this action being contemplated. After all, the child brought into your relationship is not like a warm puppy bought at the local pet store. They cannot be returned just because they whine all night or wet the floor.

Our best advice to you is before you make a parenting decision as described in this chapter, discuss it with your partner, if you have one. Then get good counsel from a mental health or family guidance professional sympathetic to your cause. Once the decision has been made to bring a child into your life and relationship, seek adequate legal counsel. Find an attorney who is experienced in family law, adoption, surrogate parenting and is sympathetic to your cause.

Good luck.

# AIDS

**H**aving a chapter on AIDS in a book on coming out to your children as a gay/lesbian parent might appear out of character to this book; however, if we consider the political nature of this disease and some of the accompanying misunderstanding and hysteria that has surrounded AIDS, we felt we would be remiss to not include some guidelines on this issue.

It is unlikely that anyone reading this book has not heard of AIDS or in fact missed the impact of this disease. Many of us have lost countless numbers of friends and colleagues over the years, so just addressing the considerations surrounding AIDS will be painful for many readers.

AIDS has been around longer than any of us knew at the onset of this tragedy. AIDS (acquired immunodeficiency syndrome) first appeared in 1981 with the death of two homosexual men, who had been otherwise healthy, but suffered a severe collapse of their immune system, then succumbed to unusual but seldom fatal illnesses. In those days there was no name for this dreaded disease; due to the target population, i.e., homosexual men, there was less (almost no) sympathy and concern.

In the struggle for a name and reason to explain this disease, the gay community, which had made a number of social and political advances over the years, began to feel the impact of this killer. Names like the "gay plague," God's revenge or wrath on gays, "just desserts to the deserving," etc., became fashionable in jokes, news and editorial headlines, political by-lines and religious justification for the condemnation of this disenfranchised minority called "gay men."

During this struggle for name and reason came blame, as if gay men created this disease, then out of boredom decided to spread it around. An excellent book on the history of this disease is *And The Band Played On* by Randy Shilts. In it he chronicles the disease before it hit this country, discloses a part of its epidemiological path through the sexual exploits of Gatan Dugas, a Canadian flight attendant who soon became known as *Patient Zero*, as the source of infection in the United States and Canada. This "phenomenon" of *Patient Zero* became the subject matter for almost every talk show. This brought on more pressure for the gay community, which has had both positive and negative results.

It is now known that AIDS has been in the United States since 1975. During this time many sexually active homosexual men served as plasma donors for Hepatitis B serum. Blood samples taken during this time were later tested, showing a surprisingly high percentage to be HIV positive. Even though this new discovery created another shock wave on how long this disease had been in this country, it was not to be the final shock. There was a case reported in the late 60's of a black teenage male who had died of an inexplicable collapse of his immune system. The doctor working on this case had the foresight to save serum and tissue samples for later testing, should this disorder ever surface again. To the shock of everyone, when the samples were tested, the results returned HIV positive!!!

As AIDS is reviewed retrospectively, most authorities agree AIDS has been around for a number of years, some say 25 years, others say over 100 years, originating in Africa either as a new virus or as an animal-to-man viral transfer that is deadly in humans but not disease-producing in certain animals. The disease then migrated to the western hemisphere through Haiti and on into the United States. So, the thing termed the "gay plague" actually is an illness caused by a retrovirus now commonly referred to as HIV (human immunodeficiency virus), that primarily attacks the immune system rendering it incapable of providing the immunological functions necessary to enable humans to fight off disease.

AIDS is primarily a venereally transmitted disease requiring the exchange of bodily fluids, most commonly semen, vaginal secretions and/or blood, during sexual contact. However, there are other known pathways of transmissibility, i.e. contaminated blood and blood products, IV drug abuse with shared contaminated needles, transmission of the virus through open wounds on the skin and through the mother-baby connection during pregnancy. There are no documented casual contact methods of transmission of AIDS; there are a handful of cases, however, for which the route of transmission is not well established.

Since the pathways of transmission mostly are known, preventative measures can be taken to avoid infection from this virus. The Surgeon General of the United States mailed guidelines to every household for protection, which included advice on abstinence from sexual contact, use of a latex condom if being exposed to body fluid sexual activity, the use of lubricants containing nonoxynol-9, sex only with committed partner, limited number of partners and continuing to use safe techniques if there is a question of your at-risk status, especially if you do not know your HIV status, but also if you do and cannot verify the sexual activity of your partner or his or her HIV status. These pamphlets are available from the Surgeon General's Office or your local health department. It is your individual responsibility to protect yourself.

This disease has been at *least* as political as it has been medical, which is more in keeping with reasons to include this information in this book. For the majority of gay men, this will be an issue brought up if you have children, want to have them or apply to be an adoptive parent. One of the most common experiences gay male parents have when they tell their children that they are gay is to have them ask some question about AIDS. Here are just a few typical questions asked: "Do you have AIDS?" . . . "Now that you are gay, won't you get AIDS?" . . . "Don't all gays have AIDS?" . . . "What if you get AIDS, what will I do?" . . . The list could go on forever. A major theme in the questions is that AIDS and gays are synonymous, one being the inevitable outcome of the other.

With uneasing frequency this question arises in many legal proceedings concerned with visitation and custody issues. Courts have been known to order HIV testing, the results of which are used to make decisions. Men occassionally have refused to take the test as a part of the trial, and have been refused access, even visits, to their children. Children known to be living with a gay parent have been required to be tested in order to remain in school. The horror stories on the resultant hysteria of this disease are endless.

For a number of years there has been much controversy about whether or not to be tested. During the early years of AIDS, the advised position of the gay leadership was to not be tested. Since in the early days there was little to nothing that could be done, test results were academic at best, leading to severe psychological consequences at worst. Since the virus causing AIDS may have a very long latency period, there may be no physical effect for many years. Most scientific minds agree that unless there is adequate medical treatment developed, it is a matter of time only (not if) until some symptoms appear. Whether this is an inevitably fatal virus still is not known; this appears to be the case, however, except for a handful of long-term survivors.

With at least some palliative measures available in the treatment of AIDS, testing has taken on new meaning in recent times. With AZT available for anyone HIV positive, with or without symptoms; with new protocols of treatment mixing AZT with antivirals and immune modulators; with the handful of experimental drugs and the knowledge that the earlier the better to start antiviral and other preventative treatment, much longer and healthier survival is being seen. There is a fair amount of optimism that this in the near future may be a chronic but treatable disease, while cures continue to be sought.

Testing, for whatever reason, can be beneficial in making your plans for the future. Testing is a very personal decision. If you are HIV negative, there probably will be a lot relief. If you are HIV positive, it may only verify what you already know or it may cause varying degrees of psychic trauma. However, testing can produce unexpected outcomes. Insurance companies carefully scan for testing or refusal to be tested. If you are applying for insurance, whether life or health, you should know if testing will be a requirement, because if you apply and later discover that requirement, then refuse, the refusal may well be fed into Medical Information Bureau, a massive computer data bank much like credit bureau services, and that red flag will haunt you forever. Many insurance companies scan medical records to see if HIV testing was done in conjunction with a health concern. Even if the results are negative and you meet a certain profile of "probably being gay," you may find your insurance being suddenly cancelled or find yourself in a cost spiral that you cannot afford. Therefore, some wisdom should go into how you are tested, who has access to these records and what will be done with the information. Anonymous testing at a reputable lab from which *you* control all of the information is probably most advisable.

If you do decide on HIV testing as a part of your decision-making on whether to try for custody or adoption, and are positive but without symptoms, you may have some tough decisions to make. You certainly will want to consider the best interests of your child, as well as consider how this might impact your ability to parent. Many people make tough decisions about having children in the face of dramatic health issues. Examples include the woman who has a slow growing but inoperable brain tumor, but chooses to conceive a child and care for her son or daughter as best she can for as long as she can. A man who has an untreatable heart condition chooses to father a child and be the best father he can for the number of years he has. It probably is obvious there is no easy answer to your question. Our best advice is to go slow, get the best and most trusted counsel available and make the decision that fits you best.

If you are considering a surrogate route for being a parent, using your sperm, you most definitely should be tested (and retested) to provide the best assurance you can of being HIV negative.

Outside the issue of custody, your HIV status can impact being a gay parent. Even if you are and remain HIV negative, if you are a gay man AIDS has probably impacted your life and may impact your child's life. As mentioned early in this chapter, many of us have lost many friends and the grief is frequently incalculable, sometimes never seeming to end before another friend gets sick and dies. Such grief is indeed a part of life; except in wartime, few of us experiences such loss in such high amounts, in such a short period of time. Except in the gay community, your grief may not receive a lot of understanding and support. In like manner, whatever level of grief your child experiences may not receive understanding and support. Sometimes just telling a friend about an AIDS death may bring on fear or condemnation of your child. If there are issues around AIDS death and dying, share this with your child. Sadly, this grief will not pass quickly.

In the event you, your partner (if you have one) or a friend becomes HIV positive, becomes symptomatic or has AIDS, this will be a very stressful time for you and your child. In fact, the whole family may well be deeply impacted. Fears and rumors abound in the best of circumstances and families. Your best ammunition is good, up-to-date, factual information. Since all written text rapidly becomes dated, time will not be taken here to outline everything you need to know. It is a good idea to bring up the subject and have open discussions about fears that may accompany the diagnosis. It is reasonable to rely on your family doctor for information. If he/she is not experienced with HIV illness or even if he is, use your local health department, AIDS resource centers and gay community information banks.

In the event you are HIV positive and become ill and have custody of your children, careful planning for their future is advisable and in order. The provisions should be made early in the illness since a significant number of AIDS patients have varying degrees of dementia which makes detailed planning difficult if not impossible. Even in the absence of dementia, many patients are so fatigued they do not think clearly, again a reason for early planning. Depending on the age of your children, it is beneficial to include them on the planning as to their wishes. In a number of cases there is no family outside the gay parent and his partner, which may raise a variety of custodial nightmares. Wills, transfer of custody and the like has already been discussed in other chapters of this book. If there is a strong desire on the child's part to remain with your partner, their "surrogate parent," a lawyer's assistance will be necessary and we encourage you to seek an attorney experienced in family law.

Even though AIDS sounds grim (and in many ways is), a number of gay men, gay parents included, have reported this as a very positive time in their lives. They have reported that after the initial adjustment to the shock of the diagnosis, they became very at peace with themselves, experiencing a new vitality in their relationships, a new way of viewing their life and experiencing a much closer relationship with their partner and children. Louise Hay has a number of books, tapes, meditations, etc. to assist in the transition with this disease. Many of these books are available at major and gay bookstores.

We certainly hold every prayer there will be rapid medical breakthroughs for the treatment and cure as well as prevention of AIDS. Our best treatment now is prevention. Arm yourself with safe sex information, THEN PRACTICE IT!

To our best knowledge, AIDS has not hit the lesbian community[1] (other than IV drug abusers); therefore, there has not been much attention paid in this chapter to our lesbian sisters. However, a tribute to that sisterhood is in order. The lesbian community has rallied to the cause. They have been at the forefront of fundraising, providing counseling, transportation, visiting and prayers for those stricken with AIDS. Many have taken their gay brothers into their homes, nursed them to the end, when all else turned their backs on people with AIDS (PWA'S). They have donated blood when gay blood bank accounts were drying up because of a lack of acceptable donors. And they have joined in the marches to protest the lack of political, social and religious support in this disease that knows no sexuality, race, sex or boundaries. It would behoove the world to take an example from the lesbian community. Lesbians come from a community where they enjoy more stable relationships than their gay brothers and their heterosexual counterparts, a community almost free of venereal disease; a community where many already enjoy rather stable parenting rights.

Few case histories dealing with AIDS have happy endings, but many PWA's live happy lives as a part of the process of going through a frightening, sometimes painful and ultimately challenging illness, from the onset of the first symptoms to the final transition.

The decision to electively bring a child into your family in the presence of an HIV diagnosis will be a difficult one at best, and requires a lot of soul searching and careful planning. The reality of this illness should be no different than any other grave illness, the outcome of which might

---

[1] At press time there are two documented cases of female-to-female transmission. The facts of this virus change everday, once again, encouraging us to be responsible and keep updated.

effect the children. There have been a number of cases dramatically presented on movies made for television, depicting a woman diagnosed with a terminal brain tumor who could still conceive and bear the child without hastening her illness, or the leukemic man who wants a progeny to carry on for him; therefore choosing to produce an heir, even though their time together will be relatively short. In the overall planning on whether or not to electively have a child in your life in the face of such a challenge should have no more or less weight in the decision making process than any other illness. Unfortunately, that has not been the case.

**Case Study**

Jay's story adequately details such a case. Jay fought a valiant struggle to get custody of his children from his wife, Ellen. He voiced a lot of concern over the children's safety if they continued to reside with their mother. He revealed their marriage was made in hell more than heaven; they met in a drug rehab center and began a shaky relationship there.

During an early session, Jay recalled their first meeting in the center, stating, "I was in a lot of pain over my addiction, my confused sexuality, having practically no family of my own and feeling an intense loneliness like I had never felt before."

He admitted the counselors in the rehab center had warned the community members not to get emotionally (romantically) involved with one another, since those kinds of relationships are usually doomed to failure anyway. Jay, however, in his bull-headed way, discounted the advise thinking, "Some relationship is better than none. After all, Ellen accepts me just as I am, even with my gay/bisexual confusion."

Jay, in some of his more lighthearted moments, chuckled at their early years together, stating, "We moved into the worst flop-house you could imagine. Just think, me, from an upper middle class background, sleeping on a mattress on the floor, no furniture, no television, just that mattress and a few scattered boxes for storage, makeshift tables, even an occasional chair if we could find a wooden box."

During the first two years they had two children, John and Mic. Jay did well with his recovery, faithfully attending meetings and working his program. He went to computer school and found he was a whiz at working out extremely complicated computer problems, and found himself catapulted into financial freedom.

Ellen, on the other hand, continued to use drugs, at first prescription, then "high quality street," then anything she could get. She was in and out of many treatment centers, always achieving a shaky recovery and soon relapsing. She and Jay frequently had arguments over her relapses and he constantly threatened to leave, citing his most major fear over her IV drug abuse and the possibility of getting AIDS. Most of the fights ended in the same way—Jay storming out of the house, going over to some gay friend's house, Ellen drinking herself into a stupor, calling her sister, Joan, to come and watch the kids, then going on a three-day drug binge. Feeling very trapped, Joan would call Jay to come home and take care of his own kids and she would go out looking for Ellen, nearly always finding her detoxing in one of the local hospitals.

After a number of years of this neverending spiral, Jay started to invite his gay friends over to the house, being rather open with his children about his friends and their lifestyle. Since there were so many unusual things about this family, having gay friends was not unusual to the kids at all. Most of these friends were men from Jay's recovery group, who were supportive of Jay's efforts to live with a non-recovering person.

During the bleakest period, when Ellen had a number of close calls with death from drug overdoses, bacterial endocarditis from dirty needles and a close bout with hepatitis, Jay became very close to one of his recovering buddies, Mike. Due to her weakened physical condition, Ellen was unable to get out to get drugs and perhaps this blessing in disguise gave her the longest "non-use" drug free time she had ever had. However, Jay began to feel like he lived with a stranger, lived in constant fear of another relapse for Ellen, and began to worry about his own ability to remain sober.

Due to the need for almost constant supervision, Jay stayed at home most of the time, being able to work from his home computer. The family, therefore, did not experience severe financial hardships, other than the drain caused by Ellen's medical bills. During their marriage Jay had remained sexually faithful to Ellen, at least physically, admitting to masturbation while thinking of men to whom he was attracted, and now especially Mike.

When it appeared as though Ellen was going to make a strong recovery from her physical problems and Jay had some hope of getting closer to her in order for their relationship to get back on solid ground, he found he had no sexual interest in Ellen. The last few times he was sexual with her, he found himself constantly fantasizing about Mike.

Jay recalls the next event with painful clarity, even to this day. He stated after more soul searching prayer and agony, he had decided to tell Ellen the marriage was over. He went over to Mike's house to rehearse the confrontation. Mike was very supportive and stated, "I don't know if I am the most objective person for you to talk to, because . . . you see . . . I think I am in love with you. Being in recovery, I did not want to get my stuff mixed up with yours, and was satisfied just being around you as a friend . . . well . . . really hoping one day there might be a chance for me . . . but . . . uh . . . you know . . . shit! This is hard, Jay. I don't know what to say and if I say more I'll just make a bigger fool out of myself."

Jay sat in Mike's living room with his eyes filled with tears. While he had much the same feeling, he did not need this now to complicate the picture. He questioned his timing to have this encounter because Ellen was away at the dentist having some minor work done and probably would not feel very good anyway. They also had just had a major argument over her returning to the same dentist who was known for his "feel no pain" philosophy, giving Ellen most anything she asked for in the way of narcotics and tranquilizers.

Taking a deep breath Jay stared Mike into the eyes,

gave him a big kiss and said, "Damm you, don't do this to me . . . .I feel the same way!!" and walked out of the house.

When Jay returned home he had decided against an encounter at this moment. Upon entering the house he could tell something was wrong. The kids were glued in front of the television set with the volume so low there was little reason for it to be on . . . which meant only one thing . . . the migraine after the visit to the dentist . . . the Demerol shot which put her to sleep . . . the huge prescription of Percodan, Valium, and Seconal (Quaalude could no longer be ordered). As Jay walked into the bathroom he saw another horror—a 10cc vial of Demerol, needles, tourniquet, used syringe still lying on the floor and all of the usual prescriptions in the medicine cabinet. In their darkened bedroom he saw Ellen passed out on the bed. He briefly checked to see if she was still breathing, which she was. He told the kids to get a few things together because they were all going to stay at Mike's for a few days. Jay then went into the bathroom, destroyed the drugs, called Joan to see after her sister, stating only, "I'm out of here!"

Jay got a few changes of clothes for himself, then called Mike. Crying, he recalled his opening statement to be something like this: "Mike, I really hope you love me like you said you do, because I need you now more than ever. I'm leaving Ellen and taking the kids with me, and I need a place to stay because I think this thing is going to get ugly. I don't want the kids caught in the middle. Ellen is in the middle of a stupor and this time I destroyed all of her stash. Boy! Is she going to be pissed off big time!"

Mike, somewhat overwhelmed with the intensity of the moment, also hoping that his best wish would come true, replied, "Of course, don't hesitate for a minute. Y'all get over here. Do you want me to call Randy (an attorney from their recovering group)?"

"Yes!" Jay shouted without thinking. "I'm such a gutless wonder, if I don't get things into motion now, there may never be another chance when I feel the courage to do what I have to do."

Jay paused on that thought, stating, "I would have never believed, and in a way still don't believe, things would have turned out this way." He further stated, "I guess I wanted . . . no, needed . . . love, attention, nurturing, in essence I needed Mike in a way I never realized. The two boys slept in the guest room, I started out sleeping on the couch in the living room, but ended up in Mike's bed. And sure, we had sex on that first night, unfortunately, not safe sex."

Over the course of the next few months things became very stormy. Ellen was served with divorce papers. During the hearing Mike petitioned the court for sole custody of the children—wanting Ellen's parental rights revoked, barring that, only the most restrictive supervised visitation. Having been given temporary custody through an action by Child Protective Services, the children continued to reside with Jay and Mike. Since a number of Mike's friends had AIDS or already had died, Ellen filed a counter motion that her children were unprotected from "potential death" and demanded their custody be transferred to her until the "safety" of the household could be determined. She also insisted on a court order requiring Mike and Jay be tested, with the absurd addendum that all gay visitors be tested if they were to have contact with the children. Since there had already been a number of HIV positive friends visit, she insisted on the children being tested.

The transfer of custody was immediately granted, the testing taken under consideration, but would be required if Jay was to challenge the transfer of custody. Jay had little fear for his risk, but remembered his first sexual experience with Mike was unsafe. Mike felt reluctant to be tested, more out of a political stance than concern for himself, yet Jay wanted to respect his wishes. In a counter move he insisted Ellen be tested due to her IV drug use, the motion being denied.

This level of arguing back and forth raged on for about one year. Jay and Mike remained together, with Jay being able to see his children only one time per month, but without physical contact. Jay decided he could not live under these restraints regarding his boys; he therefore agreed to be tested and urged Mike to do the same. Since their homosexuality had never been hidden during the divorce and in all of the custody hearings, he assumed the courts to be tolerant of lifestyle. He felt he had a chance for revised custody or a least more relaxed visitation.

Jay and Mike discussed the ramifications of testing and results. Mike realized he was at greater risk to be positive than Jay and was worried if he was positive and Jay was not, Jay would leave, especially knowing this might pave the way to a better chance in the legal proceedings involving the boys.

Jay told Mike he could make no promises. The way he felt now was they would be together no matter what the results. He also felt with time and more education the judge in the case may feel different anyway and it was not like he could not see or communicate with his sons.

On the day of the test, Jay turned to Mike and said, "There's no turning back now. Our lives may never be the same again."

Mike responded, "I know."

Awaiting the test results, the next week seemed like an eternity. The call came from the clinic saying the results were in and both were to report in for the results. As they entered the clinic the counselor stated, "Do you want to hear the results together or separately?" They had previously agreed to hear the results together.

The counselor left the room for a few minutes, again a time that seemed to never end, as Mike and Jay held each other with an ominous feeling of doom. When the counselor returned he stated, "I believe in just telling it like it is and not do any of the television drama stuff. Jay, you are negative, congratulations, continue to be safe. Mike, I'm sorry, you're positive, you have a challenge ahead of you whether you get sick or not . . . no, both of you have a challenge. I'm sorry if I seem blunt, but after doing this hundreds of time, I believe the direct truth is the best. Now you will both be advised to be retested in three months. There can be false positives and negatives, but that is rare. I will be glad to answer any questions either now or later. Sometimes right after hearing that the results are positive, words become moot. I have found that a good warm hug does a lot more than words in the initial phases."

Both Jay and Mike had tears streaming down their faces and the counselor was right. All three hugged silently for a few minutes, then all departed the office. Jay and Mike drove in absolute silence for almost an hour. Finally, Mike cried out, "You can leave me if you want. I know what we said before, but it is all different now. I'll only be in the way of you, your kids and your happiness. Besides, watching me die is no way to bring up kids or for us to have a relationship. Maybe this is the Higher Power's way of saying to do things differently."

"Bullshit!" Jay screamed. "This has nothing to do with the Higher Power. It is simply . . . complexly . . . a challenge in our lives. I am not going to leave you and am not going to give up on the kids. There just has to be a way out, but whatever it is, it has to be together."

The follow-up retesting proved to be the same, Mike positive but healthy and Jay negative and healthy. Unfortunately, the results and Jay's tenacity to stay with Mike provided more fuel for Ellen's arguments to keep the kids away from them. She further convinced the judge there was no such thing as "safe sex," she was sure they were still having sex, therefore her children remained at risk, especially since there was no conclusive proof, as far as she was concerned, that all routes of transmissions were known, and she was unwilling to take any risk.

The following three years took many unexpected turns. Mike progressively got sick, experiencing a rather rapid downhill course, dying after a short bout with pneumonia. Jay was overcome with grief, coming very close to a relapse in his drug use, but was determined to survive all this and be available to his children as their father, whatever that was beginning to mean in the presence of all this turmoil. The children were stunned by Mike's death and felt very unresolved about it, not being able to be around him because of the judge's order.

Jay, in an almost guilty way, felt some amount of relief that maybe things would change in custody or visitation. Ellen had continued to have an almost constant battle with her addiction, spending more time in relapse than recovery. Joan had become the surrogate parent and would frequently sneak the kids over to be with their father, realizing she was under no orders from the court and also feeling the orders to be absurd.

On one such sneaky visit, Joan was very strained and asked Jay to join her in the bedroom for a private talk. With a quivering voice she stated, "Ellen is back in the hospital, another relapse, which I'm sure is no news to you. She has been so bad lately, I don't know what to do. I feel that my protecting her the way I do is enabling her addiction. She is on heroin and speed, one up and one down . . . she looks terrible . . . old, drawn and she is so skinny. Well, the doctor decided to test her for HIV without her consent since she has been out of it for the week. They don't know if she is toxic or demented. She turned out to be positive. God, Jay, she has AIDS!"

Jay simply stood there, dumbfounded. Then he cried out, "Not again, I can't go through it again. Mike, now her, and what the kids will have to go through. This is almost too much!"

Mustering some courage, Joan said in a whisper, "With all due respect, Jay, I can't go through any more either. I am the one caught in the middle. These kids are not mine but I have had to be mother and father to them. I don't blame you for the asinine way the court ruled, it's not your fault. Nevertheless, everyone sounds concerned about everyone else except me. I cannot and will not go through any more of this. I know you are divorced, but you and Ellen will have to work it out."

Jay decided to go to the hospital to see Ellen. Floating in and out of a daze, Ellen replied, "Cruel irony, isn't it? I do all these things to hurt you and I end up with the big 'A'. God sure has a good aim. I guess I deserve it."

Jay was filled with both compassion and anger. His mind raced with the thoughts of Mike and was thankful the end was quick and relatively painless. He had flashes of envy of those still alive and well, in whom some treatment seemed to help. Then he looked at Ellen and struggled with what to feel. He thought honesty might help by saying, "There remains a lot of differences between us and this is no time to try and settle it. I think we need to look at our common enemy which is not our differences, rather it is AIDS. We also have a common bond, our children, and they have suffered enough. I cannot say that I love you but I do love what we have, our children, and in that there is love between us. Let's all go home when you are strong enough and see this thing through to the end. The doctors tell me your system is so weak, time will tell all. Whatever time there is, let's make it good for the kids and as good as we can for us."

Ellen struggled to have a faint smile on her face, then dozed off.

During the next six months there was much healing and still lots of pain. Ellen took the room Mike had died in, with the kids in the guest room where all of this had started years ago. Jay was on the couch, somewhat bemused with the irony of it all. The boys were old enough now to help in the letting go process. They asked many questions about how it was for Mike, why Mother got the disease since she was not gay, if they would get it because the judge forced them to live with their mother, especially when it turns out that she had been sick for a number of years.

Jay took adequate time to explain about the routes of transmission, that being an IV drug abuser was her most probable route of infection, and that they were at no risk from casual contact.

The children were also concerned with what would happen to them when their mother died. They were afraid the courts would come get them again and perhaps make them live with Joan. Jay assured them all of this had been straightened out with the courts; they would continue to live with him. He told them how easy it is for people, even though they mean well, to get hysterical about something they don't understand, and make bad decisions trying to do good things. He encouraged the boys to always ask questions if they are afraid or don't understand.

During the last month of Ellen's life, the most intense healing took place for this family. Much of the time she was almost in a coma; in her lucid moments she told the children she had been wrong in her decisions and made up bad stories to tell the judge, knowing full well just putting fear of the unknown into her story would make her win. She also helped them understand about her disease of addiction and how that had led her to getting AIDS. She encouraged Jay to take another partner when he felt like dating, trying to bring some humor into this sad situation by saying, "Check him out first . . . don't be a three-time loser."

With tears in his eyes, gently holding Ellen's hand, he replied, "I am a winner, it's just that the game is so damm hard to play."

Those were the last words between Ellen and Jay. After that she slipped into a deep coma and died that night.

Jay retained custody of his children as the surviving parent. Just prior to press time for this book, he called to say he had a new lover, a man with two daughters, and it looks promising. He said in his usual convivial way, "You know, as much as I disliked Ellen and all that she put me through, I took her advice. We were both tested and retested and are negative. She said don't be a three-time loser. All considered, I think that I am a three-time winner!"

AIDS will continue to get worse in numbers of victims, but there is hope on the horizon. Many suggestions in this text will change. Remember, it is every individual's job to be informed. Protect yourself and use good judgment!

# Helpful Resources

ll information noted in this section was obtained from indirect sources, such as switchboards, advertisements or resource lists in publications, other guides, etc. The scope of the information provided is according to their specifications. Please note that the names, addresses, and phone numbers of these resources were current at publication time.

Organizations, associations and professional resources are encouraged to submit contact information for future printings. Send listing to: Editech Press, P.O. Box 611085, N. Miami, FL 33261-1085.

## GAY PARENTS, MOTHERS AND FATHERS

Parents Support Group, Phoenix, Box 32441, Phoenix, AZ 85064

Gay Parents Group, c/o GLAD, Box 117, Tempe, AZ 85281

Gay and Lesbian Parenting Group, Berkeley, CA (415) 841-4622

Lesbian/Gay Parenting Rap, c/o Diablo Valley Community Center, 1818 Colfax, Concord, CA 94520

Parents Group, c/o Gay Community Service Center, Box 36777, Los Angeles, CA 90038 (213) 464-7000

Gay Mothers and Fathers, San Diego, c/o Gay Community Center, 1447 30th Street, San Diego, CA 92102

Gay Mothers and Gay Fathers, c/o The Gay Center, 2550 B Street, San Diego, CA 92102 (415) 863-9413

Gay Parents Group, 2131 Union Street, San Francisco, CA 94123

Parents, Lovers and Children's Group, San Francisco, CA (415) 751-1977

Gay Fathers and Lesbian Mothers, c/o GATE, Box 1852, Edmonton, Alberta, CN T5J 2P2

Gay Parents, c/o Gays for Equality, Box 27, UMSU, University of Manitoba, Winnipeg, Manitoba, CN R3T 2N2 (204) 269-8678

Gay Parents Association, c/o Gay/Lesbian Community Center, 1436 Lafayette Street, Denver, CO 80218

Lesbian Mothers and Gay Fathers, Washington, DC (202) 548-3238

Gay Parents Support Group, c/o Center for Dialog, 2175 Northwest 26th Street, Miami, FL 33142

Sexual Identity Center, Box 3244, 2139 Kuhio Avenue, Honolulu, HI 96801 (808) 926-1000.

Parents Group, c/o Gay Horizons Center, 3225 North Sheffield Avenue, Chicago, IL 60657 (312) 929-HELP

Gay Parents Association, c/o M. Connell, 930 North Broadway, No. B., Wichita, KS 67214

Gay Parents Group, c/o Steve Clemmeth, 3907 East Vernon Street, Wichita, KS 67218

Gay Parents Support Group, c/o St. Louis Community Center, 1022 Barracks Street, New Orleans, LA 70116

Parents Who Are Gay, P.O. Box 548, Colombia, MD 21045

Lesbian Mothers/Gay Fathers, P.O. Box 25, Laurel, MD 20810

Gay/Lesbian Parents of Portland, c/o F. Brooks, 26 Cushman Street, Portland, ME 04102

Gay Parents, 348 West 14th Street, New York, NY 10014 (212) 242-6616

Parents Group, c/o Dayton Gay Center, 665 Salem Avenue, Dayton, OH 45405 (614) 228-4875

Gay Parents Dallas, 3444 Normandy Street, Dallas, TX 75205 (214) 528-1024

Gay Parents Group, c/o AURA, P.O. Box 7318, Fort Worth, TX 76111

Gay and Lesbian Parent Support Group, Montrose Counseling Center, 900 Lovett, No. 203, Houston, TX 77006

Gay Parents Group, P.O. Box 1170, Seattle, WA 98111

Gay Fathers of Phoenix, Box 23004, Phoenix, AZ 85002 (602) 257-0350

Gay Dads, P.O. Box 5323, Berkley, CA 94705

South Bay Gay Fathers, 1266 White Oaks Road, No. 110, Campbell, CA 95008

Sacramento Gay Fathers, Sacramento, CA (916) 441-4594

Bay Area Gay Fathers, Box 31622, San Francisco, CA 94131

Gay Fathers Support Group, Box 283, San Francisco, CA 94101

Gay Fathers Unlimited, 625 Post Street, San Francisco, CA 94101

Gay Fathers Support Group San Jose, San Jose, CA (408) 998-3034

Gay Fathers of Santa Clara County, c/o Richard, Santa Clara, CA (408) 238-7878

Gay Fathers, c/o GRIC, Box 1828, Station M, T2P 2LB, Calgary, Alberta, CN (403) 234-8973

Gay Fathers of Hamilton, Box 44, Station B, Ontario, CN L8I 715 (807) 523-7055

Gay Fathers of Ontario, P. O. Box 187, Station F, Toronto, Ontario, CN M4Y 2L5

Gay Fathers Support Group, 435 Roehampton Avenue, Toronto, Ontario, CN M4P 1S3

Gay Fathers Coalition, Box 50360, Washington, DC 20004 (202) 548-3238

Gay and Married Men's Association (GAMMA), Box 28317, Washington, DC 20005 (202) 548-3238

Chicago Men's Gathering, Box 11076, Chicago, IL 60611 (312) 649-0730

Gay Fathers Coalition, Indianapolis, IN (317) 546-9339

Fathers in Transition, GCN Box 6, Boston, MA 02111

Gay Fathers of Greater Boston, P.O. Box 1287, Kendall Square, Cambridge, MA 02142

Don Mager, 8011 St. Paul Street, Detroit, MI 48214 (313) 824-4819

Gay Fathers Coalition, Kansas City, MO (816) 931-4470

Gay Daddies, 11-48 ½ East Street, No. 2, New York, NY 10003 (212) 431-1913

Gay Fathers Forum of Greater New York, 223 East 19th Street, No. 3, c/o Stu Gross, New York, NY 10003 (212) 460-9181

Gay Fathers Group, c/o Henry Weiss, 305 East 40th Street, New York, NY 10016 (212) 682-4167

Gay Fathers, Inc., 334 West 87th Street, No. 8A, New York, NY 10024 (212) 580-1146

National Coalition of Gay Fathers, 146 East 30th Street, New York, NY 10016

Husbands/Fathers of Central New York, Box 6452, Syracuse, NY 13217

Gay Fathers of Westchester, c/o Larry, Westchester, NY (914) 737-5004

Gay Fathers of Greater Philadelphia, Box 3872, Philadelphia, PA 19146 (215) 732-5400

Gay and Bi Married Men's Group, c/o Dignity, 250 South 12th Street, Philadelphia, PA 19107

Gay Fathers, Box 13149, Philadelphia, PA 19101

Gay Fathers Coalition, Box 1672, Newport News, VA 23601

Gay Fathers Support Group, c/o Phil Herrington, P.O. Box 22744, Seattle, WA 98122

Gay/Bi-Sexual Husbands/Fathers Support Group, c/o 15 S. First Street, #A 420, Minneapolis, MN 55404 (612) 338-0209

Lesbian Mothers Group, c/o Pacific Center, 2712 Telegraph Avenue, Berkeley, CA 94701 (415) 841-6224

Mothers And Others, 2923 Fulton, Berkley, CA 94705 (415) 549-0755

Peninsula Mothers Club, 444 Matadero Avenue, Palo Alto, CA 94306

Lesbian Mothers Group, Sacramento, Sacramento, CA (916) 456-3245

Lesbian Task Force of NOW, Box 1404, Sacramento, CA 95807 (916) 443-3470

Sacramento Lesbian Mothers, Sacramento, CA (916) 966-5116

Lesbian Mothers of Teens, San Francisco, CA (415) 626-7106

Lesbians with Children San Jose, San Jose, CA (408) 470-9687

Lesbian Mothers Support Group, Santa Cruz, Santa Cruz, CA (408) 728-9233

Lesbian Mothers Support Group, Santa Rosa, Santa Rosa, CA (707) 823-7718

Lesbian Feminist Mothers Political Action, P.O. Box 65804, Station F, Vancouver, British Colombia, CN V5N 5L3

Lesbian Mothers, c/o Lynn Fraser, 320 5th Avenue SE, No. 124, Calgary, CN T2G 0E5

Lesbian Mothers, c/o GRIC, Box 1828, Station M, Calgary, Alberta, CN T2P 2L3 (403) 234-8973

Lesbian Mothers New Haven, P.O. Box 3438, Yale Station, New Haven, CT 06520

Lesbian Mothers Group, Boston, MA (617) 524-0034

Lesbians With Children, c/o Women's Educational Center, 46 Pleasant Street, Cambridge, MA 02139 (617) 354-8807

Parents and Co-Parents Rap, c/o Daughters of Bilitis, 1151 Massachusetts Avenue, Cambridge, MA 02138 (617) 661-3633

Lesbian Mothers, Maryland (301) 251-1225

Lesbian Mothers Support Group, c/o G.C.C.B., 241 West Chase Street, Baltimore, MD 21201

Lesbian Mothers Rap Group/St. Louis, St. Louis, MO (314) 865-4623

Lesbian Mothers Group, P. O. Box 703, Princeton, NJ 08540

Dykes and Tykes Legal Custody Center, 110 East 23rd Street, No. 502, New York, NY 10011 (212) 777-8358

Lesbian Mothers Support Group, c/o Lesbian Resource Center, 713 Monroe Avenue, Rochester, NY 14607 (716) 244-8640

Lesbian Mothers Support Group, Cincinnati, OH, c/o Dee (513) 961-5934

Lesbian Parenting Alliance, P.O. Box 420496, Portland, OR 97202 (503) 224-5399

Lesbian Mothers Group, c/o Sisterspace, 3500 Lancaster Avenue, Philadelphia, PA 19104 (215) 222-5110

Lesbian Mothers Group Pawtucket, P.O. Box 755, Pawtucket, RI 02860

Lesbian Mothers Support Group, National Organization for Women (NOW), Box 40982, Memphis, TN 38104 (901) 458-1661

Lesbian Mothers, Houston, TX (713) 529-4975

Gay Wives and Mothers Collective, 57 Maide Causeway, Cambridge, England, UK

Northern Virginia Lesbian Mothers Group, (804) 734-9063

Geni Martel, 2105 Grove Avenue, Richmond, VA 23220 (804) 358-2939

Responsible Gay Mothers, c/o Lesbian Resource Center, 4224 University Way, WA 98105

## RELIGIOUS AFFILIATIONS AND RESOURCES

A Capella Chorus (Church of Christ), Box 291206, Los Angeles, CA 90029

Affirmation: Gay and Lesbian Mormons, Box 26302, San Francisco, CA 94126 (415) 641-4554

Affirmation: United Methodists for Lesbian and Gay Issues, Box 1021, Evanston, IL 60204 (312) 475-0499

American Baptist Concerned, 2418 Browning St., Berkeley, CA 94702 (415) 841-4269

Brethren—Mennonite Council for Gay Issues, Box 24060, Washington, DC 20024 (202) 462-2595

Catholic Coalition for Gay Civil Rights, Box 1985, New York, NY 10159 (718) 629-2927

Church of God Caucus for Lesbian and Gays, Box 9163, Denver, CO 80209

Conference for Catholic Lesbians, Box 436 Planetarium Station, New York, NY 10024 (212) 595-2768

Dignity Inc., 1500 Massachusetts Avenue N.W., Suite 11, Washington, DC 20005 (202) 861-0017

Evangelical Outreach Ministries, Box 7882, Atlanta, GA 30357 (404) 288-5801

Evangelicals Concerned, c/o Dr. Ralph Blair, 30 E. 60th Street, Suite 1403, New York, NY 10022 (212) 688-0628

Friends for Lesbian and Gays Concerns (Quakers), Box 222, Sumneytown, PA 18084 (215) 234-8424

Gay and Lesbian Christian Fellowship, Box 1204, Waldorf, MD 20601 (301) 888-2636

Integrity Inc., P.O. Box 19561, Washington, DC 20036-0561 (718) 720-3054

International Conference of Gay and Lesbian Jews, Box 881272, San Francisco, CA 94188

Jehovah's Witnesses Gay Support Group, c/o Jim Moon, Box 3744, St. Thomas, VI 00801

Lutherans Concerned, Box 10197, Chicago, IL 60610

National Center for Gay Ministry (Catholic), 35-17 W. Burleigh, Milwaukee, WI 53210 (414) 962-1978

New Ways Ministry (Catholic), 4012 29th Street, Mt. Rainier, MD 20712 (301) 277-5674

Orion Fellowship Alliance, Inc. (Seventh Day Adventist), Box 4768, San Francisco, CA 94101 (415) 626-6240

Presbyterians for Lesbian and Gay Concerns, c/o James D. Anderson, Box 38, New Brunswick, NJ 08903-0038 (201) 846-1510

Seventh Day Adventist Kinship International, Inc., Box 3840, Los Angeles, CA 90078-3840 (213) 876-2076

Unitarian Universalists for Lesbian/Gay Concerns, Box 1077, Back Bay Station, MA 02117-9998 (617) 522-2425

Unitarian Universalist Office for Lesbian/Gay Concerns, 25 Beacon Street, Boston, MA 02108 (617) 742-2100

United Church Coalition for Lesbian/Gay Concerns (United Church of Christ), 18 N. College Street, Athens, OH 45701 (614) 593-7301

United Lesbian and Gay Christian Scientists, Inc., P.O. Box 2171, Beverly Hills, CA 90213-2171. (213) 850-8258

Universal Fellowship of Metropolitan Community Churches, 5300 Santa Monica Blvd. #304, Los Angeles, CA 90029 (213) 464-5100

World Congress of Gay and Lesbian Jewish Organizations, Box 881272, San Francisco, CA 94188

## LEGAL RESOURCES

American Civil Liberties Union, Gay Rights Chapter, 633 South Shatto Place, Los Angeles, CA 90005-1387 (213) 385-5585. Lawyer Referral (213) 467-4141

Lesbian and Gay Center Legal Aid Program, Box 1124, San Diego, CA 92112 (619) 692-GAYS, 6-10 PM

Gay Rights Advocates, 540 Castro Street, San Francisco, CA 94114 (415) 863-3624

Lesbian Rights Project, 1370 Mission Street, 4th Floor, San Francisco, CA 94103

National Lawyers Guild Gay Caucus, 558 Capp Street, San Francisco, CA 94110 (415) 285-5066

San Francisco Bay Area National Lawyers Guild, 558 Capp Street, San Francisco, CA 94110

Gay Law Students at Hastings, Hastings College of Law, 198 McAlister, San Francisco, CA 94102

Lesbian Mothers Defense Fund, Box 38, Station E, Toronto, Ontario CN M6H 4E1

Gerald A. Gerash, Attorney at Law, 1535 Grant Street, #180, Denver, CO 80203 (303) 861-0700

Holmes, Hunter, Polikoff and Bodley, 1319 F. Street NW, Suite 1004, Washington, DC 20004 (202) 783-3410

Lesbian and Gay Rights Caucus, Antioch School of Law, 2633 16th Street NW, Box 3, Washington, DC 20009 (202) 265-9500

Rights to Privacy Foundation, Box 1723, Washington, DC 20013

Women's Legal Defense Fund, 2000 P Street NW, Suite 400, Washington, DC 20036 (202) 887-0364

Heyward and Schildmeyer, Attorneys at Law, 4834 Klondike Road, Lithonia, GA 30058 (404) 987-0455

Rene C. Hanover, One North LaSalle, No. 1111, Chicago, IL 60602 (312) 346-9690

Gay and Lesbian Advocates and Defenders (GLAD), Box 218, Boston, MA 02112 (617) 426-1350

Lesbian and Gay Parent Project, 21 Bay Street, Cambridge, MA 02139 (617) 492-2655

Lambda Legal Defense Fund, 132 West 43rd Street, New York, NY 10036 (212) 944-9488

National Lawyers Guild, Gay Rights Task Force, 835 Broadway, New York, NY 10003 (212) 260-1360

Community Law Project, 1628 SE Ankeny Street, Portland, OR 97214 (503) 233-4747

Custody Action for Lesbian Mothers (CALM), Box 281, Narberth, PA 19072 (215) 667-7508

Abby Rose Rubenfeld, Cheatham and Palmero, 43 Music Square West, Nashville, TN 37203 (615) 244-4270

Lesbian Defense Fund, Box 4, Essex Junction, VT 05452 (802) 862-9046

Gay Parents Legal Research Group, Box 1723, Lynchwood, WA 98036

Lesbian Mothers National Defense Fund, P.O. Box 21567, Seattle, WA 98111 (206) 325-2643

## FAMILY AND SOCIAL SERVICES

Federation of Parents and Friends of Lesbians and Gays, Inc. (Parents FLAG), Box 27605, Washington, DC 20038-7605 *For chapters in your locale, write this office.*

National Gay Youth Network, Box 846, San Francisco, CA 94101

Spouses of Gays, 450 Sutter Street, Suite 2100, San Francisco, CA 94109

Parents of Gays Mississauga, 3323 Kings Mastings Crest, Mississauga, Ontario, CN L5L 1G5

Spouses of Gays, c/o Caryn Miller, 204 St. Clair Avenue, West Toronto, Ontario, CN M4V 1R2

Parents of Gays, Box 9094, Ottawa, Ontario, CN K1G 3T8

National Federation of Parents and Friends of Gays (NF/PFOG), 5715 16th Street NW, Washington, DC 20011 (202) 726-3223

Sexual Minority Youth Assistance League (SMYAL), 1638 R Street NW, #2, Washington, DC (202) 232-7506

SIGMA (Spouses in a Gay Marriage), P.O. Box 262, Pella, LA 50219. *Use initials on envelopes, please!*

Straight Partners, P.O. Box 943, Addison, IL 60601

Straight Partners—Spouses Anonymous, P.O. Box 6191, South Bend, IN 46660

Straight Partners, Box 1603, Hyattsville, MD 20788

Family and Friends of Gays of Rochester, Box 601, Fairport, NY 14405 (716) 266-1247

Parents of Lesbians and Gay Men, P.O. Box 553, Lenox Hill Station, New York, NY 10021 (914) 793-5198

Gay-Straight Partners Alliance, 810 East 29th Street, Eugene, OR 97405

Spouses of Gays, Philadelphia, PA (215) 288-6959

National Gay Alliance for Young Adults (NGAYA), P.O. Box 190426, Dallas, TX 75219-0426

Families and Friends of Gays and Lesbians, 5336 Northeast 184th, Milwaukee, WI 53205

Family and Children's Services of Minneapolis, Lesbian and Gay Counseling Program, 414 S. Eighth Street, Minneapolis, MN 55404 (612) 340-7444

## HEALTH AND RELATED SERVICES

West Hollywood Cares, 8512 Santa Monica Blvd., West Hollywood, CA 90069 (213) 385-5585

Pacific Center for Human Growth (counseling), 2712 Telegraph Avenue, Berkeley, CA 94704

Open Quest Institute (counseling), 3803 Udell Court, Los Angeles, CA 90027 (213) 664-5000

Fae Panner, L.A. Women's Therapy Center (counseling), 12581 Venice Blvd., Los Angeles, CA 90066

Margery Shelton, M.S.W. (counseling), 1401 Sanborn Avenue, Los Angeles, CA

The Sperm Bank of Northern California, Feminist Women's Health Center, 2930 McClure Street, Oakland, CA 94609

David L. Lundquist, L.C.S.W. (counseling), 683 North Calle Marcus, Palm Springs, CA 92262 (619) 323-8025

George Deabill, M.S. (counseling), Box 11363A, Palo Alto, CA 94306

Timothy Wolf (counseling), 2423 Camino Del Rio South, Suite 111, San Diego, CA 92108

AIDS Hotline, San Francisco, CA (415) 863-AIDS

Bay Area Physicians for Human Rights (BAPHR), Box 14546, San Francisco, CA 94114 (415) 673-3189

Lyon-Martin Clinic, 2480 Mission Street, San Francisco, CA 94110

Midwives Alliance of North America, San Francisco, CA (415) 653-9930

National Mobilization against AIDS, 2120 Market Street, San Francisco, CA 94114 (415) 431-4660

Operation Concern (counseling), Box 7999, San Francisco, CA 94120 (526) 563-0202

Gay Counseling Group, The Bridge (counseling), 640 Campus Drive, Stanford, CA 94305 (415) 497-3392

Brian Miller, M.F.C.C., Ph.D. (counseling), 8235 Santa Monica Blvd., Suite 307, West Hollywood, CA 90046 (213) 660-4495

National Lesbian/Gay Health Foundation, Box 675472, Washington, DC 20009 (202) 797-3708

Society for the Psychological Study of Lesbian and Gay Issues, American Psychological Association, 1200 17th Street NW, Washington, DC 20036

Gay Horizons Community Center (counseling), 3225 North Sheffield Avenue, Chicago, IL 60657 (312) 929-HELP

Andrew Mattison, Psychologist (counseling), 814 Blackhawk Drive, Park Forest, IL 60466 (312) 534-2470

Gay and Lesbian Counseling Service, 80 Boylston Street, Suite 855, Boston, MA 02116 (617) 542-5188

Miriam Rosenberg, M.D., Ph.D. (counseling), Boston, MA (617) 358-7512

Joseph Lamott (counseling), 24 Elm Street, Suite 10, Westfield, MA 01086

Tod Bergman, M.S.W. (counseling), 324 Garden Street, Hoboken, NJ 07030 (201) 798-8289

National Association of Social Workers Task Force on Gay and Lesbian Issues (referral resources and bibliography), 110 West State Street, Trenton, NJ 08608 (609) 394-1666

Peer Counsel (counseling), Box 812, Santa Fe, NM 87501 (505) 983-5598

E. Sue Blume, C.S.W. (counseling), Hempstead, Long Island, NY (516) 483-7883

Charles Puglisi, Ph.D. (counseling), Box 161, Middle Valley, NY 11379

Association of Gay Psychologists (referrals), 210 Fifth Avenue, New York, NY 10010

Gloria Back, C.S.W. (counseling), 135 East 83rd Street, Suite 4D, New York, NY 10028 (212) 861-6998

Gotham Psychotherapy Associates, New York, NY (212) 903-4033

Robert Gould, M.D. (counseling, expert witness), 144 East End Avenue, New York, NY 10028 (212) 535-7275

Homosexual Community Counseling Center, 30 East 60th Street, New York, NY 10022 (212) 688-0628

Identity House (counseling), 544 Sixth Avenue, New York, NY 10011 (212) 243-8181

Institute for Human Identity, Inc., 490 West End Avenue, New York, NY 10024 (212) 799-9432

Audrey Steinhorn (counseling), 110 West 86th Street, New York, NY 10024 (212) 799-9190

Richard Green (counseling, especially with children of gays; expert witness), SUNY at Stoneybrook, Nicolls Road (HSC Mega-structure), Stonybrook, NY 11794 (516) 444-2581

National Gay Health Foundation, Box 834, Linden Hill, NY 11354

National Gay Health Education Foundation, Suite 1305, 80 Eighth Avenue, New York, NY 10011

AIDS Hotline, New York, NY (212) 685-4952

Association of Lesbian and Gay Psychologists (AGLP), 210 Fifth Avenue, New York, NY 10010

National Association of Lesbian and Gay Counselors, Box 216, Jenkintown, PA 19046

Eromin Center (counseling), 412 South 16th Street, Philadelphia, PA 19146 (215) 732-3212

Paul G. Powell, M.S.W. (counseling), 1041 South 6th Street, Philadelphia, PA 19147 (215) 334-3343

Andre "Rip" Corley, C.S.W., A.C.P. (counseling, expert witness), 3570 Vancouver, Dallas, TX 75229 (214) 357-2371

Vicki Morris, RN, M.S.S.W. (counseling), 1033½ Bishop, Dallas, TX 75208 (214) 631-5217

Oak Lawn Counseling Center, 2017 Cedar Springs, Dallas, TX 75201 (214) 520-8108

Lesbian, Gay and Bisexual People in Medicine, 1910 Association Dr., Reston, VA 22091

Poseida Institute Counseling Center, 1945 Laskin Road, Virginia Beach, VA 23454 (804) 425-0715

Pepper Schwartz (researcher, expert witness), Department of Sociology, DK-40, University of Washington, Seattle, WA 98195 (206) 543-5872

Seattle Counseling for Sexual Minorities, 1505 Broadway, Seattle, WA 98122 (206) 329-8737

Gay Counseling Services, 3707 West Michigan Avenue, Milwaukee, WI 53208 (414) 342-2729

Feminists Self-Insemination Group, Box 3, 190 Upper Street, London N1, England, UK. *Write for book on self insemination.*

## CHILDREN'S SERVICES

Children of Gays, 8306 Wilshire Blvd, Suite 222, Beverly Hills, CA 90211 (213) 738-1088

Children's Rights Inc., 3443 17th Street NW, Washington, DC 20010

International Institute of Children's Nature and Their Rights, 1615 Myrtle Street NW, Washington, DC 20012

Mountain Meadow Country Experience, 3736 Kenawha Street NW, Washington, DC 20015. *Summer camp for children of lesbian mothers.*

Children of Lesbians and Gays, c/o Noel Maze, P.O. Box 12501, Fort Wayne, IN 46863

Boys of Lesbian Mothers, 953 West Broadway, Eugene, OR 97402

A Note on the Book

This book was edited by Jean Chang
of the Publications Staff
of Editech Press of Miami, Florida.
Special thanks to William Edmondson
for editorial and promotional guidance.
The text was set in Bookman.
Sandra Mesics of Dark Horse Press
designed and set the text.
Vicki Sarasohn designed the cover.
R.R. Donnelley & Sons of Crawfordsville, Indiana
printed and bound the book, using paper
manufactured by the Glatfelter Company.